25 10-Minute
From
Actors Theatre of
Louisville

SAMUEL FRENCH, INC.
45 WEST 25TH STREET   NEW YORK 10010
7623 SUNSET BOULEVARD   HOLLYWOOD 90046
LONDON   *TORONTO*

— Foreword —

The ten-minute play, like speed chess and the fifty-yard dash, is something of a secret. What you are unlikely to know if you haven't worked with the genre is that the energy that can be generated is enormous, and that it can lodge like a sliver in the mind of a viewer to remain for a lifetime.

How is this possible when character and plot are squeezed by the vise of the form? Well, it tends to illuminate moments of profound change and realization. It doesn't usually lead to the glancing blow but the knockout punch. It has teeth and claws as a satirical delivery system. Its very limitations often lead away from strict realism and its authors seem unabashed in going for the big statement. It has a cocky, aggressive, rueful tone that charms. It has a win, lose, who cares attitude that tends to leave prudence in the dust. I like it.

As an actor's or director's teaching tool, it's plainly valuable. These pieces have, in the main, been commissioned for young actors so that they can deal with structure, character and theme while playing parts of their own age. These short works demand much of the preparation a longer role might take, but have the advantages of minimal production requirements and shorter rehearsal periods.

For the young actor, they make demands but don't overwhelm. For the young director, they create the panoply of tasks and responsibilities in miniature. For the young playwright, they show the mechanism like seeing the watchworks through a glass case. As classroom work, in my opinion, they beat scene study hollow because there is no referring to parts of a play you aren't producing. They are a whole, albeit a small whole.

You can produce eight of them and delight an audience; you can produce one of them and allow a classroom breakthrough; you can read all of them and learn more about the craft of playwriting than you ever thought possible.

Plus, they can tell a story that forty minutes or two hours would have ruined, and we've all gotten stuck with *that* guy at a party.

> — Jon Jory
> Producing Director
> Actors Theatre of Louisville

TABLE OF CONTENTS

Spades
A short play

by
Jim Beaver

SPADES a short play by Jim Beaver

It is a condition for the production of this play before any public audience that the following notice be prominently displayed in all advertising for the play and prominently posted in the theatre lobby and/or box office:

SPADES CONTAINS STRONG, REALISTIC LANGUAGE AND DEPICTIONS WHICH MAY BE OFFENSIVE TO SOME PEOPLE

1st PRODUCTION FEBRUARY 18, 1981

DIRECTOR	Larry Deckel
LIGHTS	Jeff Hill
SETS	Paul Owen
COSTUMES	Kurt Wilhelm

All programs and printed publicity material for this play must carry the following notice:

CORPORAL JACK CHITWOOD	Brian Keeler
LANCE CORPORAL ROB FLANAGAN	Timothy Busfield
YOUNG MARINE	Kent Broadhurst

DEDICATED TO
Jerry Cooper
and all the other boys in the back room

COMMISSIONED AND FIRST PRODUCED BY ACTORS THEATRE OF LOUISVILLE

CAST

CORPORAL JACK CHITWOOD, USMC, 22
LANCE CORPORAL ROB FLANAGAN, USMC, 19
YOUNG MARINE
RADIO VOICES (5 male, 1 female)

SETTING

Place: Graves Registration warehouse, 1st Medical Battalion, 1st
    Marine Division, Da Nang, South Vietnam

TIME

2300 Hours (11 PM), October 5, 1970.

AUTHOR'S NOTE

SPADES is designed to stand alone or as the second piece in a pairing with its companion play *SEMPER FI.** If paired, there should be no break between the two plays, the helicopter roar at the end of *SEMPER FI* serving as a transition into the beginning of *SPADES.*

Several words of either military or Vietnamese derivation are given correct pronunciation and definition in parentheses immediately following the words' appearances in the script. It should be noted that the word "beaucoups," though French, has entered the Vietnamese language with its meaning, but not its pronunciation, intact. Americans who mimicked the Vietnamese variation pronounced the word "boo-koo," rhyming exactly with "cuckoo."

Chitwood and Flanagan may be dressed either in Marine regulation camouflage trousers (note that Marine and Army camouflage differed), boots, green t-shirt, and Marine utility cap, or in the more casual clothes common in Vietnam, even in work situations: camouflage running shorts, "B.F. Goodrich" sandals, and militaresque t-shirts with slogans. The utility cap, however, would ALWAYS be worn outdoors, even in casual clothes, and the taking it off and putting it on would be second nature whenever going in or out.

---

*Contact author's agent, Triad Artists, for details.

Spades

AT RISE: Darkness. The crushing roar of a helicopter beats down, then fades into the distance. The lights come up on one end of a warehouse containing a table and two chairs, a small, half-size refrigerator, a military field telephone, and a transistor radio. On one wall is an American flag and a yellow-on-red sign reading "1st Med Bn, 1st Mar Div, Body Shop." On the table are cards, crossword puzzle books, a butt kit (coffee can ashtray — olive drab), and a copy of "Mila 18" by Leon Uris. A large stack of crossword puzzle books is on the refrigerator. There are two doorways, one upstage, leading to the cooler room. Fading in with the lights is the sound of a radio.

RADIO VOICE #1. . . . said to be despondent over the recent deaths of musicians Jimi Hendrix and Jim Morrison, whose deaths were also linked to possible drug abuse. However, no official cause of Miss Joplin's death has been announced. Once again, singer Janis Joplin, dead at 27. That's the news for this hour. Repeating the hour's top story, the Pentagon announced today that for the third straight day, there were no combat-related deaths in Vietnam (rhymes with bomb, not clam).

(Coinciding with this last statement, Enter JACK CHITWOOD, 22, and ROB FLANAGAN, 19, sweating like pigs and dressed as per the author's note. They carry a stretcher with a blanket-covered body on it. The corpse's face is disfigured by the dogtag jammed between its upper incisors for identification. They carry the body into the cooler room and (offstage) place it in a cooler drawer. They re-enter, then exit the way they came in, taking the stretcher with them. They repeat the operation with another dogtagged body, this one uncovered and wearing a blood-soaked camouflage uniform. They return a third time with a body completely covered (including head), this return timed to coincide with the first song heard on the radio. The RADIO VOICES continue throughout this routine.)

RADIO VOICE #1. *(continues)* . . . This is Army sergeant Richard Muldoon reporting the Twenty-three Hundred edition of AFVN news for the Armed Forces Radio Network. *(electronic sign-off music)*

11

RADIO VOICE #2. This is AFVN, the American Forces Vietnam Network, serving the American Fighting Man 24 hours a day, from the Delta to the DMZ. With studios and transmitters in Quang Tri ("Kwong Tree"), Da Nang ("Duh Nang"), Qui Nhon ("Quinn Yon"), Pleiku ("Play Koo"), and Nha Trang ("Nuh Trang"), and key network stations in Saigon, Vietnam.

RADIO VOICE #3. Hey, Bill, I just heard Joe's got the clap!

RADIO VOICE #4. (*laughing*) What! That's great! (*combined laughter*)

RADIO VOICE #5. It may be funny when it happens to Joe, but what if it happens to you? The clap is no laughing matter. Your unit medical officer can give you full instructions about the prevention and treatment of venereal disease. So don't be the Joe that everyone's laughing at. See your medical officer today.

RADIO VOICE #6. (*female very sexy*) Welcome back to Vietnam Showcase. I'm Chris Lamarr, with your favorite music till Oh-Three-Hundred hours. This next song goes out to all the guys in Comm. Company, One-One, on Hill Ten. So for all you Marines, and all the other fellows who've made this the most requested song in Vietnam, here's The Animals, and "We've Gotta Get Out of this Place."

(**Song plays. JACK and ROB Enter with their covered stretcher-load, a single dogtag lying loose on top of the blanket.*)

ROB. Wait a minute, Chitwood. This guy's dogtag is loose.

JACK. Well, set him down and fix it. Damn corpsmen, can't trust them Navy guys to do nothin' right. (*They set the stretcher on the floor.*)

JACK. Well, are you gonna do it?

ROB. I never done it before. I don't know how.

JACK. It's simple. You pull his jaw down, slide the dogtag in edge-wise in the little notch between his front teeth, then give him a good kick in the jaw, hard enough so the tag gets wedged in nice and tight. That's all there is to it.

ROB. I can't do that. I don't mind carryin' 'em around, but I can't kick him in the jaw.

JACK. Why not? He won't feel it.

---

*Cautionary note: Permission to produce this play does *not* include permission to use this song in productions.

Rob. Yeah, but I will.

Jack. Okay, if you're gonna be a puss, I'll do it myself. . . . (*JACK picks up a half-drunk soda from the table, swigs, and rubs the cool can over his forehead.*) Turn off that radio, will ya? I been hearing that song twenty times a day for almost a year now. I'm sick of it. (*ROB does so, then continues marking notes on a clipboard.*) If it ain't that one, it's "Mr. Lonely" or "Comin' Home Soldier." Must think we're a bunch of masochists out here. (*JACK puts down the soda and bends by the stretcher. He pulls the blanket away slightly, though we do not see what he sees.*) Well, looks like them corpsmen didn't forget after all. Look at this, Flanagan.

(*ROB walks over, looks, cringes with a sick scowl.*)

Rob. Aw, shit, Chitwood! What'd ya show me that for? You're sick.

Jack. Ugly fucker ain't got no jaw to wedge it in. Come on, let's get him in the cooler. . . . Is this our stretcher?

Rob. No, it belongs over at the LZ.

(*JACK and ROB take the body into the cooler. JACK comes out, calls back to Rob.*)

Jack. You finish tagging him, and I'll run this back over to Receiving.

(*JACK Exits with the empty stretcher. After a moment, ROB comes out carrying a black plastic bag, its semi-liquid contents weighing about 5 lb. He places it in the small refrigerator which contains a case or two of sodas. ROB sits and begins working a crossword puzzle. JACK enters and fills clipboard forms.*)

Jack. Saw Langfeldt over at the LZ. He wants to know if we want to get a game up.

Rob. I wouldn't mind playing some cards, but not with Langfeldt. He can't play for shit. When I was in his section, we used to play 25–30 games a day, and after three months, he still didn't know that when you're playin' spades, spades is the only trump.

Jack. Yeah, I played a couple of games with him and them other guys at the comm shack this afternoon. In one of 'em, ol'

Langfeldt went nolo, and then what does he do? Throws down the ace and the king of spades. On a nolo bid!

ROB. He's dinky-dao, man. Beaucoups dinky-dao. (*"Boo-koo dinky-dow": crazy, real crazy.*)

JACK. Well, if you don't want to play with him, maybe we can get some other guys over here.

ROB. Maybe later. I wanna finish this crossword.

(*JACK cools himself again with his soda can. He sits, bored, especially since ROB's concentration is trained on his crossword puzzle.*)

JACK. D'ya hear about Joplin dying?

ROB. (*not looking up*) Yeah. That's a bitch, man. She was a damn good singer.

JACK. Yeah. I saw her in San Diego last year with Big Brother and Steve Miller and Chicago Transit Authority. She was great.

ROB. Just 27, I heard. That's a drag, man, dyin' that young.

JACK. Yeah . . . (*JACK finishes his soda and gets up to get another one.*) You want a soda?

ROB. Yeah. Gimme a root beer.

(*JACK goes to the reefer, gets out two sodas, notices the plastic bag.*)

JACK. Hey, what's this bag in here? That's not what I think it is, is it?

ROB. It's that bag of partials we got in this afternoon.

JACK. And what the fuck's it doin' in here? I don't want no bag of guts in the same place I keep my food!

ROB. It was taking up a whole cooler drawer, and I didn't have no place to put that last guy we brought in.

JACK. There's sixty-five fucking drawers in there!

ROB. Yeah, all full. So what'd you want me to do, leave that whole stiff out here to bloat while that little bag took up a whole drawer?

JACK. Well, you didn't have to stick it in here with our food!

ROB. Aw, now who's bein' a puss?

JACK. Well, I'll find someplace for it, but it ain't gonna stay in my reefer. (*JACK takes the bag to the cooler. ROB turns back to the crossword. JACK returns, sits, reads. A roach the size of an Almond-Joy half scuttles across the floor. JACK jumps up and stomps it.*) Gotcha! (*JACK takes a notepad from his pocket and makes a mark in it.*) I'm still ahead of you. I bet I break two thousand if they don't rotate me home early.

ROB. King of the Roachkillers! You been here longer'n me. I coulda killed two thousand roaches easy in the time you've been here.

JACK. Crap! It's all over the bottom of my boot.

ROB. (*looking at the mess*) That was a big one.

JACK. It's a baby. When I was up at An Hoa ("Ann Wah"), we had roaches so big they'd steal C-Rations right outa the box.

ROB. How could roaches get into a can of C-Rats?

JACK. Easy. . . . One on the can, two on the can-opener.

ROB. Bullshit. . . . What's a seven-letter word that means chest structure?

JACK. (*beat, then a serious suggestion*) . . . How about "titties?"

ROB. (*really considers it, then—*) . . . No, it's gotta have a G in it. Wait a minute. Starts with a R.

JACK. (*confused*) R-G?

ROB. R, blank, blank, blank, blank, G, blank.

JACK. Chest structure, huh? . . . (*thinks, then with certainty*) Ribcage.

ROB. Yeah! R, I, B, C, A, G, E. And that makes 26 – Down — Aw, hell, this ain't no fun. I can still read half the answers where I erased them last time.

JACK. Well, then, why don't we call some guys and play some spades?

(*Before ROB can answer, we suddenly become aware of a growing noise from the cooler room, a noise which quickly becomes a terrible racket, with muffled moans and shouts. JACK and ROB jump up and look at each other wide-eyed.*)

ROB. Jesus! What's that?

JACK. Holy Shit! One of them guys ain't— (*Before JACK or ROB can take more than a step toward the cooler, a demon from hell comes screaming out of the cooler room. It is a pale, bloody young marine, twisting and fighting, screaming "I'm dead! I'm dead!" over and over again through his teeth which are clamped bloodily around his own dogtag. JACK and ROB struggle to control the flailing, horribly wounded man, but he dodges and wrestles them with incredible agility and strength. His screams of "I'm dead!" combine with the following lines of JACK and ROB to form a terrifying chaos. Over action.*) Easy, fellow, easy. It's okay. You're okay! You're not dead. You're okay (etc.).

ROB. (*simultaneously*) You're not dead, man! It's just a mistake. You're gonna be all right. Listen, man, it's okay! You're not dead (etc.).

JACK. (*over the man's shouts*) Flanagan, let's get him to Receiving, he's cracked up!

(*JACK and ROB finally get a good hold on the marine and steer him toward the door.*)

ROB. Come on, fellow, let's go. You're gonna be all right.

JACK. You're gonna be all right, okay? (*JACK and ROB support the man out, his shouts of "I'm dead!" fading. A few moments pass before JACK and ROB return. Scared, breathing heavily.*) Can you believe that, man? Goddamn corpsmen! Goddamn corpsmen! They woulda let that guy get buried alive! Those guys would fuck up a wet dream!

ROB. Hey, man, we didn't notice he was alive, either.

JACK. That's their fucking job, man! Ain't ours! How are we supposed to know they sent us a live one?

ROB. (*catching his breath; then, a new thought*) Oh, man. It's too bad they didn't catch it before they tagged his teeth.

JACK. (*grimacing*) Ooo, yeah. (*shivering*) Oooooo!

ROB. (*shivering and laughing*) Ooooooo!

(*The laughter grows from shivering nervous chuckles into full-blown belly-laughs.*)

ROB. (*laughing hard*) Jeez, that scared the shit outa me. I'm STILL shakin'.

JACK. (*laughing hard*) Me, too. I thought I was gonna have a heart attack, man! I thought, oh, shit, it's a fuckin' ghost come to get us!

ROB. (*imitating Frankenstein walk*) "I'm dead, I'm dead, I'm dead!" (*JACK and ROB stagger with hysterical laughter. They calm down, then break out again. Finally:*) Funny, us working around all these stiffs all the time and then getting the shit shocked out of us by a live guy.

JACK. Oh, Jeez, I gotta pee.

ROB. I think I already did. (*The field phone rings. ROB an-*

swers, struggling to hide his laughter. Standard phone greeting.)
First Med Battalion, Graves Registration, Lance Corporal Flanagan speaking, sir. . . . Oh, hi. . . . Yeah. . . . You're kidding!. . . . Yeah, okay.

JACK. What is it?

ROB. (*into phone*) Hold on a second, Ski. (*To JACK:*) It's Lepinsky at Receiving. You won't believe this.

JACK. What, they got another Permanent Routine for us?

ROB. It's a Perm, okay. It's that live dead guy. He's dead again.

JACK. What? Let me talk to him. (*into phone; loving this*) Lepinsky, this is Chitwood. Why don't you guys make up your minds? . . . (*laughing*) Yeah. Well, you just make sure he's dead this time. I'm getting tired of carrying him back and forth. . . . Yeah, okay. . . . Yeah, we was just talkin' about that a while ago — before the zombie attack. . . . (*ROB again does Frankenstein. Into phone.*) Okay. See ya in a minute. (*hangs up*) Well, let's go get him again. (*JACK heads out, but ROB stops him.*)

ROB. Okay, but let's take one of our stretchers, so we don't have to make two trips.

JACK. Right. (*JACK goes into the cooler room, talking all the while, and brings out a stretcher which he unfolds.*) Ski promised me they're sure this time. Definitely a Permanent. Said if the guy gets up one more time, Ski'll buy all THREE of us a case of beer. Oh, grab the cards. Ski says they was ready to play some spades.

ROB. Hope he knows trump better'n he knows dead guys.

JACK. Well, if he don't, we'll just get the dead guy to play for him. Let's go.

(*JACK and ROB Exit as the lights fade to black. Janis Joplin's "Piece of My Heart"* comes up loud.*)

THE END

---

*Cautionary Note: Permission to produce this play does *not* include permission to use this song in production.

Bread

by
Andy Backer

BREAD by Andy Backer

1st Production May 28, 1985

Director. . . . . Robert Spera
Lights. . . . . Janine Silver
Sets. . . . . .Paul Owen
Costumes. . . . . Stephanie Saft

CAST

The MAN. . . . . LOUIS DiVINCENTI
The WOMAN. . . . . CORNELIA EVANS

SETTING

A room.

All programs and printed material for this play must carry the following notice:

FIRST PRODUCED BY ACTORS
THEATRE OF LOUISVILLE

Bread

by Andy Backer

Scene: A room. A table and four chairs. On the table is a cloth-wrapped parcel. There's a kitchen knife. There are four clean plates.

Darkness.

AT RISE: A MAN enters with a lamp, sets it on the table, and unwraps the parcel. He reveals a partial loaf of home-baked bread. He sits and looks at the bread for a moment. He looks at the door. He takes the knife and cuts off a slice of bread. He is extremely quiet. He places the piece of bread on one of the plates. He sits and stares at the bread. He turns off the lamp. He eats the bread by moonlight.

A WOMAN Enters after the MAN has eaten the bread. Only a few crumbs are left on his plate. He quietly stands up before the WOMAN is entirely in the room and can see him. She is dressed in a night dress and has on slippers. A warm blanket is wrapped around her shoulders. She sees the MAN. She sees the table, the bread, the crumbs on the plate. She says nothing.

MAN. I thought I heard something. (*She looks at him.*) I thought there was someone in here. I heard something.

WOMAN. (*Waiting a bit, then with a sigh:*) I thought I heard something, too.

MAN. I thought someone was in here. (*Trying to think of something else to say, pauses, and then continues lamely.*) I heard something, and I thought someone was in here.

WOMAN. I heard it, too. (*She picks up the plate with crumbs and brushes it clean.*) But, it was probably nothing.

MAN. (*relieved*) It was probably nothing.

WOMAN. It was probably outside. (*Sets the plate down.*) Come to bed. You'll catch cold walking barefoot.

MAN. (*looking out a window*) Yes, it was probably something outside I heard. (*turning to her*) I thought it was in here.

WOMAN. (*with a shrug*) The tree always scrapes the screen when it's windy. It was probably the wind.

MAN. It was the wind! It was windy all night!

WOMAN. Yes.

MAN. It was probably the wind! (*pause*) The tree always scrapes the screen when it's windy.

WOMAN. It was the wind.

MAN. Uh-huh.

WOMAN. What else could it be? Why would anyone want to break in? There's nothing here to steal.

MAN. No.

WOMAN. They wouldn't steal the bread.

MAN. No.

WOMAN. Not our last loaf.

MAN. No.

WOMAN. Oh, how stupid of me! (*turning on the lamp*) The bread!

MAN. The bread?

WOMAN. I forgot to wrap it! You married a dumbbell!

MAN. It's unwrapped!

WOMAN. What a klutz I am! How forgetful!

MAN. Yes . . . it was . . . forgetful.

WOMAN. Well . . . Since it's unwrapped . . .(*picking up the knife*)

MAN. (*unnerved by the knife*) What?

WOMAN. (*slices a piece of bread from the loaf*) We'll eat.

MAN. Eat?

WOMAN. Come.

MAN. The bread?

WOMAN. Sit.

MAN. But . . .

WOMAN. Eat. (*She puts the slice in his plate.*)

MAN. (*pause*) And you?

WOMAN. (*She slices off another piece and puts it in her plate and sits.*) Eat.

MAN. The kids.

WOMAN. They'll eat tomorrow.

MAN. There's no more flour.

WOMAN. You'll find work. (*Pause. He stares at the bread in his plate.*) Eat, man . . .

MAN. But . . .

WOMAN. Eat.

MAN. (*He looks at her. She doesn't look away. He slowly sits. He touches the table. Hunger eventually wins and he nibbles on the bread.*) Good. It's so. . . good! . . . (*He loses control and is soon wolfing down the re-mainder. She watches him, wraps the blanket around his shoulders, then puts her slice of bread in his plate.*) What . . . ? What are you doing?

WOMAN. Eat.

MAN. But . . .

WOMAN. I can't eat nights. My stomach won't take it.

MAN. But . . .

WOMAN. Eat. I'll eat tomorrow.

MAN. (*pause*) Yes. (*He starts nibbling on the bread.*) You'll eat tomorrow.

(*She watches him eat as the lights fade to black.*)

THE END

Attack of the Moral Fuzzies

by
Nancy Beverly

ATTACK OF THE MORAL FUZZIES
by Nancy Beverly

1st Production May 28, 1985
Director . . . . Kenneth Washington
Sets . . . . .Paul Owen
Lights . . . . Janine Silver
Costumes . . . . Hollis Jenkins-Evans

CAST

BETHANN SHUMWAY . . . . .CORNELIA EVANS
RAMON . . . . .DINK O'NEAL
MISS LOWENTHAL . . . . DONNA HARRISON
DAVE ARMSTRONG . . . . DOUG WERT
JOLLEEN BUDGE . . . . .LINDA MARGULES
ELAINE HENSELMEIER . . . . KELLY McBRIDE
SPINELESS IDIOT . . . . STEVE BECKER
BENNIE KINCAID . . . . .KEVIN READ
NADA IVANHOE . . . . RAYE LANKFORD
CLAIRICE WHITE . . . . PATRICIA FRONTAIN

SETTING

A stage.

All programs and printed material for this play must carry the
following notice:

FIRST PRODUCED BY ACTORS
THEATRE OF LOUISVILLE

Attack of the Moral Fuzzies

AT RISE: Somber Voice (In darkness): Do you feel lost? Indecisive? Queasy? Are you a stumbler in the dark? Flailing your arms hopelessly, hitting your head against unseen walls? Are you tossing and turning on the stormy sea of life, miles from a harbor of safety and calm? (pause) Relax, Beth. Come with us. No more indecision. No more guilt. Life made simple. Join us as we play the dream of your choice, MORALITY MADE EASY!!! And now, here's your host, Ramon!

(*Zippy music, bright lights — blinking lights if available — as RAMON, our sleazy host sweeps in. His able-bodied assistant, MISS LOWENTHAL, runs around throwing confetti, balloons, the whole number. Note: RAMON is not necessarily of Spanish decent; accent is optional.*)

RAMON. Good evening, good morning, good grief, Good God, great gosh almighty, hot diggity dog, come on in, sit right down, we're here, you're there, and our contestant, BethAnn Shumway is *on the spot!* (*She Enters or lights rise to reveal her. She has put on her nice Sunday outfit to come down here. She smiles nervously. She simultaneously wants to be here and wants not to mess up.*) Say Hi, BethAnn!

BETHANN. Are we on?

RAMON. We're always on, dear, that's one of the problems. Life just won't let up, will it, Miss Lowenthal?

MISS LOWENTHAL. It's just one darn thing after another.

RAMON. But today we're going to take away all of that trauma. Won't that be wonderful?

BETHANN. Yes, it will, Ramon.

RAMON. I'll bet you're glad you came to visit us.

BETHANN. Yes, I am.

RAMON. Now about those rules: millions and zillions of 'em, entirely too complicated to understand. If we understood the Rules of Life,

(*Everybody:*) we wouldn't have to play the game.

Ah, the Game, the Game she is simple. Five fun-filled rounds, each more pleasant than the last, each hinging on you unhinging that conscience. And after each one, we hook you up to the old

27

Anxiety-o-meter* to see how you're doing. Yes, how fast can you get to Nirvana, or as we like to call it, Okey-Dokey-Land. Just to see where we are, let's take that first preliminary reading. Miss Lowenthal, if you would do the honors. (*MISS L has already gotten the meter, or effortlessly escorts BETH to a contraption. RAMON does a trumpet fanfare.*) Doooo doo doo doo doo dooooooooooo . . . a nine and a half! (*SFX: taped groans*) Beth-Ann, for heaven's sake, come away from that thing. What in the world is causing all that trauma?

BETH. Huh?

RAMON. (*stage whisper*) This is the part where you tell us about yourself.

BETH. Oh. well, I work in a hospital in a cancer ward where I counsel families of dying patients.

MISS L. God, that must be terrible.

BETH. Yeah, it's really depressing.

MISS L. How do you get through it all?

BETH. I don't. Some days I just stay in bed and cry all da—

RAMON. Well, BethAnn, it's time to get rolling, time for Round One: (SFX: *ding*) International Follies. Ready? You're buying a new car. Do you purchase Japanese because it has a better performance record . . .(*Lights up on a poster of a Japanese car.*) or American, to support the home auto industry? (*Another car poster. Thinking music. SFX: ding.*)

BETH. Japanese?

RAMON. Okay, Miss Lowenthal, let's see who you've got there! (*MISS L pulls a curtain or lights reveal DAVE.*) Dave Armstrong!

DAVE. (*eager, freshly scrubbed face*) Thank you, BethAnn for helping support my dad's Toyota dealership. Because of people like you, both Japanese *and* American workers can stay employed—like my dad and me and my brother Dwayne—and also you've helped keep free enterprise alive. Thank you very much, BethAnn. (*He Exits or lights go out on him. MISS L leads applause.*)

MISS L. Very good, BethAnn. . . .

RAMON. How does it feel to have made the right choice?

BETH. I, I . . . feel pretty good.

RAMON. Ladies and gentlemen, she feels pretty good; how good is pretty good? Let's check that out scientifically with Mr. Meter. A seven and a half, very nice BethAnn.

---

*pron. anxietyOM-eter

MISS L. Very nice, BethAnn.

RAMON. I think she's on a roll, so let's get to the Second Round right now. (SFX: *ding*) Funding Mania. It's time to divvy up the tax pie. There is only enough money for keeping either Basic Grants to college students . . . (*ELAINE appears.*) *or* providing Day Care to working, lower-income moms. (*JOLLEEN appears.*) Which do you choose? (*thinking music.* SFX: *ding*)

BETH. I guess I'd provide the Day Care.

RAMON. Okay, Miss Lowenthal, who have we got this time? (*Lights brighten on JOLLEEN.*) Jolleen Budge!

JOLLEEN. (*a little stiff and camera-shy*) Thank you, BethAnn, for thinking of us. Because of your thoughtfulness, I am able to keep working at the Tastee-Freeze and still keep Wanda Sue at the Day Care Center where she receives excellent looking-after, and then I still have enough money left over to buy new tires this year. Thank you again, BethAnn.

(*BETH has noticed ELAINE Exiting, but MISS L and RAMON have maneuvered her attention to matters at hand. Applause.*)

MISS L. Awww, I feel so warm and wonderful. How about you, BethAnn?

BETH. I, I feel terrific.

RAMON. Piece of cake, isn't it?

MISS L. Easy as pie.

BETH. (*shaking the tension out of her hands*) Boy oh boy, this is so nice. You know, I used to have this little knot right back here (*points to her shoulder blades*), but it's disappeared!

RAMON. And what's the ol' Meter telling us now?

MISS L. It's a good one. Five and a half. She's heading right for Okey-Dokey-Land.

RAMON. Jolleen's happy, Dave's happy, I'm happy, you're happy, BethAnn's happy, the guys in the booth are happy, the parking lot attendant's happy, one big happy family! Round Three —

(*During RAMON's digression BETH's eyes have strayed back to where ELAINE Exited.*)

BETH. Everybody?

RAMON. Sure! Round —

BETH. Uh, Ramon, could I ask one quick question?

RAMON. I wouldn't if I were you.

MISS L. Questions really mess things up.

BETH. I was just wondering . . . does that girl get to go to college, now that she doesn't have a Basic Grant?

RAMON. I believe you're straying from our guidelines, dear.

MISS L. No worrying allowed.

BETH. I'm not worrying . . . exactly. I was just curious. (SFX: *a loud buzzer goes off.*)

RAMON. (*To the booth:*) What was that? (*identical buzzer sound*) I'm sorry, BethAnn, we have a ruling from the judge. You *are* worrying.

MISS L. Tsk, tsk, tsk.

RAMON. Don't do it, BethAnn.

BETH. This is just a little thing, no big deal. Could I just, you know, chat for a second?

RAMON. What would Mr. Meter say?

BETH. (*She's torn.*) Well . . . (*scurries off*) it'll only take a second. Where is she, back here?

RAMON. (*sings, under his breath:*) "Every party has a pooper . . . (*MISS L joins him*) . . . that's why we invited her, party pooper. . . ."*

(*BETH Enters dragging ELAINE, who is quite confused.*)

ELAINE. What's going on?

RAMON. Oh, not much. Welcome to *my* nightmare! We're making it up as we go along — BethAnn Shumway, meet Elaine Henselmeier. (*MISS L half-heartedly tosses a bit of confetti.*)

BETH. Hi, I was just wondering, do you get to go to college now?

ELAINE. I've already been — for a couple of years, in business. But I could only go part-time because I had to work. At that rate, it was taking me eight years, so I quit and got a full-time job as a receptionist in a doctor's office.

BETH. Are you going back some day?

ELAINE. I doubt it. This job's okay —

BETH. But you're probably not challenged —

ELAINE. You can't have everything —

BETH. — But this isn't fair —

ELAINE. Yeah, but I'm engaged, and my finance's got a good job selling aluminum siding —

---

*CAUTIONARY NOTE: Permission to produce this play does *not* include permission to use this song in production.

BETH. I'll give you the grant, you can have the grant—

RAMON. Ahhhhh!

JOLLEEN. (*off*) Wait a minute! (*She enters.*) You gave me the money—

ELAINE. (*To BETH:*) Really? Can you really do that?

JOLLEEN. No, she can't.

ELAINE. If I hurry, I could register for summer session.

JOLLEEN. But what am I gonna do with Wanda Sue?

DAVE. (*Entering*) Hold on, does that mean she can renege on us, too?

ELAINE. It's her decision, she can do whatever she wants.

DAVE. Indian Giver!

BETH. Oops.

RAMON. Oops, she says.

BETH. Ramon, I don't think I'm cut out for this.

RAMON. Beth, you're thinking too much. The name of the game is Morality Made Easy, not Life's a Bitch. Miss Lowenthal, paint her that picture when she makes it through all five rounds.

MISS L. Mid '70's with a warm southwesterly breeze, iced tea on the veranda, Sarah Vaughn on the stereo, reading the Sunday paper. . . .

RAMON. When was the last time you got to read *all* the Sunday paper—and didn't have to worry about what was in it? It can be yours. (*BETH takes a deep breath and mouths an "okay."*) Round Three (SFX: *ding.*) Hospital Hijinx. At a famous hospital, the writing is on the wall. Funding is being cut back. Out of these three hot ticket items, which one would you support: heart transplants for adults, liver transplants for cute kids under the age of six, or medicare supplements to keep pace with the cost of living.

(*Music starts, then slows down as if the electricity has been pulled. BETH quavers, knees buckle.*)

BETH. I can't do it, Ramon, it's too close to home. I think I'd better just throw in the towel.

RAMON. We've been at this, what, Miss Lowenthal, a mere eight minutes and already she's pulling out?

RAMON AND MISS L. QUITTER. (*BETH shrinks.*)

RAMON. You know what happens to people like you, don't you? Huh? HUH? (*BETH feeling like a five-year-old, shakes her head no.*) You become a misshapen, spineless idiot, incapable of even the most elementary decisions. Miss Lowenthal! (*MISS L* reveals a hunched-over male, à là the Elephant Man, with normal, albeit whiney, speech. And indecisive clothing.)

IDIOT. (*as if by rote*) I am a misshapen, spineless idiot, incapable of even the most elementary decisions.

RAMON. This is a man who is also paralyzed by thinking and caring too much. He could once decide which countries should have the bomb, whether we should be backing the Nicaraguan Contras, and even who could or could not have an abortion. Now he can't even pick out the color of his socks in the morning.

MISS L. Isn't that tragic, BethAnn? He could end up with red socks and a brown suit.

IDIOT. That's a nice dress, BethAnn.

BETH. Th-thank you.

IDIOT. I like that color.

BETH. Uh, thanks.

IDIOT. Actually, gray's my favorite color.

BETH. Oh. Mine's —

IDIOT. No, brown's my favorite, no, black's my favorite, no, plaid's my favorite, the cut of that dress is really dorky, BethAnn, but the shoes are nice, except they don't match, well, they *almost* —(*BETH is duly impressed.*)

BETH. All right!

RAMON. So, you see, you have to choose, it's a given. Otherwise. . . . (*He gestures to IDIOT.*) Miss Lowenthal? (*He gestures for her to gently remove the IDIOT out of his direct eyesight.*) Recapping Round Three: heart transplants, liver transplants, or medicare supplements. (*fast music,* SFX: *ding*)

BETH. (*in one breath:*) I want the largest chunk for the medicare patients, they've paid into the system the longest, and I want the second largest chunk for kids' liver transplants because it's not their fault they were born with a bad liver, and I also want money to go for heart transplants because they seem to be having a lot of success with that recently.

RAMON. (*pause, eyes her*) Covered those bases, huh, kid? Okay, Miss Lowenthal, let 'er rip. (*BENNIE KINCAID is revealed. He's sweaty, greasy, nervous, and desperate. He's an auto mechanic.*) Meet Bennie Kincaid!

BENNIE. BethAnn, how could you do this? The hospital bills are gonna kill us. Dad had insurance, but when they found out he had Hodgkin's disease, well, they aren't so friendly any more. And he's only sixty-five, so this could drag on for a long time. I'm tryin' to run the Shell station by myself, and when Dad comes home from the hospital, who's gonna take care of him 'cause Mom's gotta work? We just aren't quite keepin' up with the cost of livin', BethAnn. The increase wasn't enough.

RAMON. Meet Nada* Ivanhoe!

(*NADA is the warm, nurturing type. She, too, is angry, but cooler about it. She speaks in modulated tones — with a veneer.*)

NADA. Hello, BethAnn. How are *you*? Have you had a nice day today? Have you enjoyed the bountiful spring weather we've been having? I don't mind telling you we're having a hard time enjoying it at the Ivanhoe home. In fact, we're not even at home most of the time. We're at the hospital with little Justin. The closest we get to spring is looking out his hospital window. As you may know, Justin is awaiting a liver transplant. If he does not receive a new liver within the next two weeks . . . (*she trails off*) Well. We, too, like Mr. Kincaid, are a little strapped for cash. The hospital was hoping to provide six free transplants this year. As you may know, funding did not quite come through. (*pause*) But we're still praying. (*pause*) I think I hear some chickadees outside. How lovely. (*pause*) Have a nice day, BethAnn.

RAMON. And finally, Clarice* White!

CLARICE. BethAnn, unlike Bennie and Nada, I am speaking for myself. I am dying. They just found out I have terminal heart disease. I am only twenty-three years old. I used to raise flowers for the 4-H. I used to be a cheerleader. I used to work as a dental hygienist. No more. Research on heart disease like mine needs to be done. (*A TV ad:*) Only *you* can help. Give to the heart foundation of your choice. A young heart is a terrible thing to waste. Goodbye, BethAnn.

BETH. I quit, I quit, I quit, I quit, I quit, I quit. . . .

IDIOT. (*loping up to her*) If that's what you want to do —

BETH. No, I *want* to make the right decision —

IDIOT. Then don't quit —

BETH. But I keep messing up —

IDIOT. That's okay —

BETH. No, it's not!

---

*pron. Nāda

---

*pron. Clair-eesé

IDIOT. Then it's not okay —

BETH. No!

IDIOT. Which cereal should I have for breakfast?

BETH. *No*!

IDIOT. Which shower curtain should I buy?

BETH. *No*!!

RAMON. So. Beth. What's up?

BETH. I messed up Round Three. I didn't make the right choice, did I?

RAMON. Are you kidding? You waffled, you fudged, you hedged, you wanted to please everyone. You and Congress.

MISS L. I tell ya.

RAMON. Well, BethAnn Shumway, looks like the game is over. (*MISS L hums "The Party's Over" for a few bars.*)

BETH. But, but, but. . . . (SFX: *the buzzer goes off again.*)

RAMON. But?

BETH. Prizes, what about prizes? You kept promising prizes! (*buzzer again*)

RAMON. You hear that?

BETH. Y-yes.

RAMON. It means you're too tense for prizes.

BETH. (*desperate*) Well, how about . . . *consolation* prizes, like a car, or a stereo, or —

RAMON. Whoa, whoa, no, no, Beth, sweetheart. There is no consolation here. We were offering peace of mind. We were offering the smug satisfaction that you'd made a good decision without second thoughts. And *you* turned it down. Prizes? If you're lucky, you'll get out of the studio in one piece — that'll be *your* prize.

(*MISS L tosses the last of the confetti on BETH. She and RAMON leave BETH alone, center-ish. The rest of the cast comes down, one at a time, to chat with BETH, slowly at first. BETH looks understandably wary.*)

CLAIRICE. BethAnn, perhaps I was a little fuzzy; heart disease is —

NADA. (*a little louder than CLAIRICE*) BethAnn, I thought you'd get a kick out of seeing Justin's birthday pictures. (*shows them*) Right now he's an off-yellow color, about the shade of my bath towels at home, but —

BENNIE. BethAnn, my dad's room number is 612, and I know he'd be real happy to see you, 'course he—(*and the push is on, they begin to converge, overlapping dialogue*)

ELAINE. BethAnn, I've already got thirty-five hours out of the way, and my grades were fine, I—

DAVE. Look, BethAnn, my dad retires in ten years, and then the dealership's mine, but there's gotta *be* a dealer—

JOLLEEN. Uh, BethAnn, I don't have any pictures of Wanda Sue with me, but she's real cute, she's two and a half—

NADA. Yes, but she isn't sick—

JOLLEEN. Well, no, but there's a lot of things I need to get her and if—

CLAIRICE. BethAnn, some people clog their arteries because of their pathetic lifestyles, but *other* people—

BENNIE. BethAnn, my dad didn't do anything to bring on cancer, he doesn't drink, he—

ELAINE. Do we have to keep talking about illness? Let's talk about something more pos—

NADA. BethAnn, Justin won't get to kindergarten much less college if he—

DAVE. I have sold used cars for four fucking years—

ELAINE. Hey, try aluminum siding—

CLAIRICE. Or laying in bed all day—

JOLLEEN. Or making ice cream cones—

NADA. Or living in a hospital ward—

BENNIE. Or pumping gas—

(*Pandamonium is breaking out. Ultimate nightmare. The IDIOT comes up to BETH. He barely gets his mouth open.*)

IDIOT. BethAnn, what should I—?

(*BETH screams, above it all, causing them all to back off from her. Lighting goes from nightmare back to reality.*)

BETH. (*with grim determination*) My favorite color is yellow, my favorite cereal is Raisin Bran, I am buying Japanese this time, and the money goes to Medicare. (*Pause while they all stare— they can't believe she made a decision. They all shrink away from her, half numb. She lashes out at them—and herself.*) What did we all want, huh? Warm breezes and iced tea? Easy answers?

People should not come on this show—I hope it dies in the ratings.

(*She storms out quickly. Lights fade. In the ATL production, we brought up Lovin' Spoonful's "Did You Ever Have to Make Up Your Mind?"* as closing music.*)

THE END

---

*Cautionary Note: Permission to produce this play does *not* include permission to use this song in production.

Eating Out
by
Marcia Dixcy

EATING OUT by Marcia Dixcy

1st Production May 17, 1988
Director............................. Marcia Dixcy
Sets.................................Paul Owen
Lights............................... Lynn Lefkoff
Costumes............................Kevin McLeod

CAST

CHRISS........................ PAMELA STEWART
MELANIE....................... HEIDI SWEDBERG
PAT............................. WENDEE PRATT

CAST

CHRISS   20's, very thin, an anorexic
MELANIE   20's, medium build, a bulimic
PAT   Late 20's, an all-American girl

SETTING

Very simple. Each woman sits in a spotlight. Each may have a small table beside her, if you wish. Pat may smoke.

All programs and printed material for this play must carry the following notice:

Eating Out

CHRISS. I haven't always been thin. People just assume that. They assume that I'm lucky. I can eat anything I want while they just have to look at food to put on weight. I feel like saying, "Obviously you're doing a lot more than looking." And I . . . can't even imagine eating anything I'd want. Kind of makes me sick to think of it. When I was in high school, all I wanted to be was petite and blonde. Instead, I was dark, dark and skinny and intense. I have one high school picture where I look exactly like something out of Aubrey Beardsley. So that was my persona, at least until I got to college. There, the world began to change. And I was reading anything that would make sense out of it. Every week, a new philosophy. Somewhere between Existentialism and Phenomenology, I guess I began to lose faith. Structures began to give way; decisions became more complex. Anyway, eating became an important comfort—a communal obsession. One true thing about women's college is the freshman ton. Collectively, every freshman class of 250 gains a ton. And that's probably a low estimate. So, I didn't play tennis, and I wasn't really in the ballpark with some of the incredible brains, and pretty soon, I wasn't even skinny anymore. Sex? (*laughs*) You know, I was so God damned scared. Let's not even talk about losing my virginity. First time out, I got vaginal warts. So I thought, forget it. This is just too much pain, too much pain. So, it was about that time, about the time when large grey areas began to overpower the black and whites, that I embarked on my first real diet. And I was very serious. I made a serious list: no fats, no fried foods, no pizza, no desserts, no bread, no cookies—my entire food intake up to that point. And of course a diet like that would work. You know, the Behaviorists say there's an optimum schedule for positive reinforcement so that you can train animals or humans to do anything. So, I guess that's what I did. That's how I trained myself to starve.

MELANIE. There are always rituals. The days you get through and the days you know you'll probably eat. Not meals. I almost never eat a meal. These rituals are alone, and they're usually late—later than you'd want a meal. Sometimes just at the point when you think you might go to bed—without. And usually, you pretend it'll just be one thing, and that will be all. But from that moment on, it seems open-ended and nothing stops it. The telephone can ring, the doorbell — you just get rid of them. Because you're racing, and you don't want to be interrupted. If you have to wait too long for the toaster, you start on cereal: bowl after bowl, and then from the box. 'Course, you have to undo your clothes — forget the jeans. Pretty soon, you take them off and cover yourself with something huge. You know, like those dogs that have the big collars around their necks that stick out about a foot so they can't bite at some hurt they have? You just divorce your body. You separate your mouth from it. And your mouth can go on forever.

PAT. I've tried it all: fasting, puking, laxatives, jogging, aerobics; it's a full-time job. I suppose the next thing will be plastic surgery, liposuction. From what I've read that'll be the wave of the future. And I remember my grandmother telling me that her mother seriously considered having her two lowest ribs removed so she could cinch her corset in tighter. Apparently, there was really a craze for that. So, some things don't improve. But there are ways to make it easier. Some you can live with, and — some you can't. And I remember the best, really the best for me was in capsule form. It's virtually impossible now, but 7 or 8 years ago you could still manage to get Control II drugs. At that time I had met a medical student and he knew this resident and we worked out a cooperative system. The resident would write me a prescription. You see, they needed me because they said it would be most unusual for these diet pills to be prescribed for a man. Seems strange, since those doctors really thrived on 'em — particularly mixed with alcohol. But Norman, this medical student, and I would drive outside the city — I was in college in Washington D.C. — and we would find these smallish towns and I would go in and get the drugs: biamphetamines, they were called. Black beauties. The first time I had one was on a Sunday: a biamphetamine brunch. And to this day, I remember that afternoon, the intensity and the power. The power to keep on going — without sleep, without food. We took this marathon bike ride. I don't even like bike-riding, really, 'cause the cars drive me crazy. But on the speed, it felt like I could pedal right off the earth, right off the rim of the horizon. And it was over 48 hours before I ate anything.

CHRISS. I had elaborate strategies to keep myself from eating. One more hour, make it through one more hour, and then the next. When I did eat, it was always exactly at the same time of day—my entire life had to be organized around that. And I always ate exactly the same things. Lettuce—large platefuls of lettuce, broth, vegetables—raw vegetables, and hard-boiled eggs—sometimes just the whites. I read somewhere that hard-boiled eggs had less calories in them than they took to digest, and, combined with grapefruit, they could actually metabolize fat. (*laughs*) Eventually, I ate all my meals up in my room. Alone.

MELANIE. Part of the deal is you keep drinking water and you keep alternating things. Like the cereal, the granola, which is sweet. I eat that in and out with bagels, bagels with muenster cheese, lettuce and mayonnaise. The whole time, I always keep track of the calories in everything. They're on the package, or the box, or on the bag of bagels. Since the mayonnaise is by the tablespoon, and I don't exactly use a whole tablespoon every time, I figure, you know, just let it go. But when you finish almost a whole box of granola and 3 or 4 bagel cheese deals, we're talking thousands of calories. It gets kind of surreal. You feel—superhuman—I don't know.

PAT. For awhile, I only took one, once a week. I'd get pretty wiped out, depleted for a few days after. I mean, it's like the adrenaline is coursing through your body, probably burning up about twice the calories. And the weight just really dropped off.

CHRISS. I weighed myself constantly, but since I was drinking so much water and Tab, I was always one or two pounds heavier than I wanted to be. First it was 125, then 115. Then I had to work a little harder so I took up swimming. I swam late in the afternoon before dinner because when I got out of the water, I knew that would be the point in the day when I weighed the very least. And every ounce I lost encouraged me to eat that much less.

MELANIE. By that time, it's all really expanding in your stomach, which is totally distended, pretty uncomfortable. And then, you start thinking about how to soothe it. I guess what you'd call the classic cure is Haägen Däzs ice cream. Anyone knows how fast a pint of that can go. Long as you got that mental collar round your neck, it goes right down.

PAT. Pretty soon it actually got kind of difficult to buy the pills. By that time, I had lost about twenty pounds. It was in the summer, you see. So we'd have to wait until a rainy day and I could wear a big slicker thing with a lot of sweatshirts under it so nobody could see my body. Still, the pharmacists who did fill the prescription for weight loss had to figure something was screwy. I thought I looked good. But my friends—one of them told me later that my face looked like a skull. Bone and skin. It was what I'd always fantasized about. That and dating a doctor.

CHRISS. My clothes became a kind of joke—huge clown pants which I'd belt in way above my waist. I went to try on other clothes. Any clothes that fit me made me feel—fat. In the dressing rooms, I always felt so discouraged. One doctor later told me that sometimes people are trapped inside the wrong bodies. They have no idea what body they really have. There are thin people who're trapped in fat bodies and they'll wear anything—tight jeans, whatever, because in their minds they look terrific. But I was just the opposite. I was a fat person trapped in a thin body. And no matter what anyone said, no matter what I weighed, or how sharp my hip bones protruded through my skin . . . or my vertebrae, or my ribs, no matter how delicate my wrist, I would always be too fat.

MELANIE. With ice cream you need something warm, to kind of melt it. Tea, maybe peppermint tea. Next you want something salty; popcorn, if you're desperate, or chips, if you've thought ahead. Maybe dip. Then it depends on what's around—chocolate, something from the freezer, you know, biscuits, or spinach souffle, or poundcake. You might not even wait for it to thaw.

PAT. I felt like I'd discovered a new twist on the fountain of youth: a prescription substitute for nourishment and sleep. So why wasn't everybody taking it? Pretty soon I was up to a pill every other day, eating and sleeping half as much as the rest of the world. What I found out was all this extra energy didn't come in the capsule. The speed just releases certain chemicals stored up in your body, and supplies of those are limited. To put it simply, whatever chemical my nervous system needed to transmit its messages got used up. And I knew I was really going haywire. For one thing, I got the chronic shakes. It became impossible to sit still in almost any situation. So I started not showing up for stuff. I think people began to find me pretty weird and unpredictable. Finally, one day, I bit right through my lower lip—bit a hole right through the middle of it.

CHRISS. It was a year before I told anyone that I'd stopped menstruating. That just seemed a blessing.

MELANIE. I wish I was exaggerating. I often think about my mother, or God, or whoever might be watching. And it's like there you are, stepping off some kind of cliff, and you do it because you know it isn't real. No one else is out there. And tomorrow, it'll all be gone.

PAT. That was that, man. I took the last bottle of pills and dumped it. Norman was really pissed at me later, but at that point, I just wanted them gone. It was a week before I could really sleep. Then, I was out for days. Afterwards it was like reentry into the normal world. Nothing felt quite the same, no instant enthusiasm. And the weight, you know at first, it was fun to gain a little back, but then it was the same old drag.

CHRISS. What finally happened was I went to give blood. You know, "A pint's a pound the world around." What I didn't know was that to give a pint of blood, you have to weigh 110 pounds. I was pretty far below that . . . I weighed 94. And there were other things. I was always freezing and there was this hair growth —this facial hair. It all got kind of out of my control.

MELANIE. I always know, because I've always checked, exactly what I weighed before, what I weighed even an hour ago. Sometimes, I've gained as much as ten pounds, sometimes more. I have a big plastic bowl. I keep it under the sink with the sponges and disinfectants there. I take it into the bathroom and set it right on my scale. And, I get on my hands and knees, I mean you know what way *you* have to do it. But I guess, at first, it pretty much has to be your fingers, at least for most people. At some point, you can train yourself and then, it's just a matter of muscle control.

PAT. There've been a few times since then, I've bought those over-the-counter diet pills. But no. They're just massive caffeine and a stomach ache. They don't really tempt me. No . . . it's hard.

MELANIE. It can go like crazy at first. I mean, ice cream is easy, but other things, like chocolate, are really harder, and—it's will power then. But I won't stop until the scale is right—exactly the right weight—give or take whatever for the bowl. So, I fill it up until I'm rid of it, completely rid of it. And then it's over. So, I always wash the bowl, take a shower, and go to bed.

CHRISS. But that's the thing about control. When you lose it, you realize how hard it is to get it back and when you get it back, the most frightening thing in the world is the thought of ever losing it again.

MELANIE. When I go out to dinner I can start to feel this panic. I mean, I try to avoid it if it ever comes up—even with my family.

PAT. I like the procedure where they wire your mouth shut. Sort of like braces to straighten out your self-control.

CHRISS. I often say I've just eaten a huge lunch. People tend to feel guilty if I tell them I'm dieting.

PAT. Otherwise, you're stuck with the same old excuses.

MELANIE. It's my stomach — really giving me trouble today.

PAT. I'm cleaning my system with fluids.

CHRISS. No, I'm allergic to animal fat.

MELANIE. Basically, I'm a vegetarian.

PAT. Too wound up to eat right now.

MELANIE. I'll have something later when I get home.

CHRISS. I could just have a bite of yours.

PAT. You go ahead, I'll enjoy it.

CHRISS. But, I'm really not that hungry.

PAT. And, I'm really not that hungry.

MELANIE. 'Cause, I'm really not that hungry.

THE END

Après Opéra

—An Opera Bouffe—

by

Michael Bigelow Dixon

and Valerie Smith

Après Opéra

—An Opera Bouffe—

by Michael Bigelow Dixon and Valerie Smith

1st production December 14, 1987
Director................................ Marcia Dixcy
Sets............................... Robert T. Odorisio
Lights.............................Michael Milkovich
Costumes............................ Susan Snowden

CAST

KAREN............................ WENDEE PRATT
PETER......................... CHRIS BURMESTER
DUNCAN................................ AL PROIA
LAUREL........................ PAMELA STEWART

Characters

PETER.................. Mid-twenties, rumpled, unshaven
LAUREL....................... 20, "Waitress from Hell"
KAREN................. Mid-twenties, dressed for success
DUNCAN................ Mid-twenties, he tries very hard

Setting

Après Opéra is a fashionable eatery with an opera motif.

Sound

Operatic choruses and arias underscore the entire play—augmenting the appropriate tragic and comic moments. The selections change as the moods in the play change.

Time

The present.

All programs and printed material for this play must carry the following notice:

FIRST PRODUCED AT ACTORS
THEATRE OF LOUISVILLE

Après Opéra

SCENE: *A fashionable eatery.*

AT RISE: *In black we hear an aria from "Pagliacci." The lights come up on PETER sitting at a table for two in Après Opéra. PETER studies a box of matches, toys with it, then pulls a match out. LAUREL, dressed in a colorful opera costume, Enters and watches PETER as he lights the match, stares at the flame, licks his first finger and thumb, and tries to squeeze out the flame.*

PETER. Owwww-shit! (*PETER sticks his finger and thumb in a glass of water.*)

LAUREL. Guess we can't all be G. Gordon Liddy.

PETER. What? Oh, no. It's an experiment. I'm testing the limits of my mind over matter.

LAUREL. That should help with our menu. Here. Can I bring you anything from the bar?

PETER. No thanks. I'll . . . uh . . . wait for my friend, thanks. Oh! Are you an opera buff?

LAUREL. Sorry. I just work here. I don't live the theme.

PETER. Oh. Would you mind asking someone then, what's the name of the opera that's playing?

LAUREL. Yeah maybe. If you're good.

PETER. Thanks . . . uh . . . Cathy.

LAUREL. It's not Cathy. I just borrowed her outfit.

PETER. Looks good. (*LAUREL Exits.*) Waitress from hell. (*PETER returns to matches and tries the same trick with other hand. Same result.*) Owwww-shit! (*Enter KAREN, looking for PETER.*)

KAREN. Peter? Is that . . . Oh, god! Peter!

PETER. Hello, Karen.

KAREN. Peter! It's so good to see you. Let's take a look. Tch-tch. You look terrible.

PETER. I'm OK. You look good, Karen. Real good.

(*DUNCAN Enters and hovers unseen nearby.*)

KAREN. You know I still think about you. Every time I eat a cookie, really, there's Peter.

DUNCAN. Like Proust.

PETER. Excuse me?

DUNCAN. "Remembrance of Things Past." (*pause*) The book? (*pause*) You know, the teacake?!?

KAREN. Honey, you're trying too hard.

PETER. Do you know this guy?

KAREN. Do I know this guy?! We're getting married on Sunday. Duncan Durbin meet Peter O'Connell.

DUNCAN. Heard an awful lot about you.

PETER. Try to ignore the awful part. Karen exaggerates.

KAREN. I do not. Come on, let's sit down. (*They look at table for two. Pause.*)

DUNCAN. If the music stops, we can play musical chairs.

KAREN. Honey . . .

DUNCAN. I'll go get another chair. (*DUNCAN Exits.*)

KAREN. So how have you been?

PETER. (*playing with matches*) Oh, OK. And you?

KAREN. What can I say? I'm getting married. But I've been dying to see you and when Duncan said he'd like to meet you, too — I talk about you all the time, what we did together — and I thought, hey, why not! Let's all get together, you know. My past and my future. We can all just be friends.

PETER. We weren't ever friends.

KAREN. Yes we were.

PETER. We were lovers. It's different.

KAREN. It's semantics. We mean the same thing. Change of topic.

(*DUNCAN arrives with chair and sits.*)

DUNCAN. So, Pete, Karen tells me you bake cookies.

PETER. Not exactly.

DUNCAN. That's what you . . .

KAREN. No, Duncan. I told you Peter manages the Cookie Nook in the mall, where they make the best chocolate fudge raisin pecan.

DUNCAN. No kidding. What's your secret?

PETER. Water.

DUNCAN. Really.

PETER. It's a mix.

DUNCAN. Oh . . . interesting.

KAREN. Honey, you're trying too hard again.

DUNCAN. Ahhh-hgth-hgth-hgth-hgth . . . (*DUNCAN drops face down on the table.*)

PETER. Jesus Christ!

KAREN. Oh dear . . .
PETER. What's the matter?
KAREN. It's all right . . .
PETER. Is he dead?
KAREN. SHHHH. Don't panic. He's OK.
PETER. Oh, sure. He looks great to me!

(*KAREN periodically attempts to sit DUNCAN upright and straighten his tie during the next few pages. He always falls back down.*)

KAREN. No, really he is. He's just a touch narcoleptic. And every once in awhile he does this, don't you Dunc? See? Breathing normally. Nothing to worry about. Let's just ignore him.
PETER. Ignore him?
KAREN. In a little bit he'll wake up refreshed and everything will be fine. Except maybe a bruise on his forehead. I should've moved that fork.
LAUREL. (*Enters*) What's his problem?
KAREN. Nothing. He's fine. (*DUNCAN falls forward again.*)
LAUREL. I can do that Heimlicher thing if you want.
KAREN. No thanks.
LAUREL. CPR?
KAREN. No, really.
LAUREL. Just checking. 'Cause sometimes people get embarrassed. And pretend nothing's wrong when there obviously is.
KAREN. It's nothing like that.
LAUREL. (*rolls eyes*) OK. Does anybody besides me need something to drink?
KAREN. We'll each have a glass of wine.
LAUREL. And for you, perhaps something flaming?
PETER. Very funny. A bourbon and soda.
LAUREL. All right. That's a B&S for the pyromaniac and a wine each for the corpse and the merry widow. (*LAUREL Exits.*)
KAREN. He does get some strange reactions.
PETER. Look, Karen. When you called last week, out of the blue, I didn't . . .
KAREN. Oh damn!
PETER. What?
KAREN. Duncan goes to this clinic where they chart his brain waves, and they shove these, you know, electrodes into his head. And sometimes they forget to pull them all out. (*She yanks a long*

electrode out.) Can I borrow your napkin? (*She applies napkin to DUNCAN'S skull.*) Thanks.

PETER. Look, Karen. . . .

KAREN. I'm sorry. You keep getting interrupted.

PETER. Well, it's just . . .

DUNCAN. Hrmufllermphf . . .

KAREN. (*after a pause*) Go on.

PETER. Well, I don't understand why you . . .

DUNCAN. HRMUFFLERMPHFFFFF!!

PETER. Is he all right?

KAREN. Oh sure. He's just dreaming. Want to see something fun? Oh, I'm sorry, you were talking.

PETER. Never mind.

KAREN. No, no. We don't have to . . .

PETER. No, just go on, OK? Please. Go on.

KAREN. OK. Watch this. Duncan? Duncan? You're strolling at night. The wind's blowing—Phewwwou. (*DUNCAN reacts with muffled sounds and movements at various points in the story.*) You went out for Hostess Ding-Dongs. (*like bell:*) Ding-dong. Ding-dong. But now you're in a cemetery. Suddenly up from a grave reaches a vampire who grabs you by your shoe. An incredibly hideous vampire with one eye, bad breath and no ears. You try to pull free but you can't. He's got you by your shoe, now your calf, now your knee. He's reaching up your thigh, now higher, higher. He's going to bite! (*DUNCAN gasps and grabs tablecloth in his fists.*) But wait! You grab hold of a vine and you pull yourself up, up, out of the grave until you're almost free. But no! The vine snaps, and you fall back into the grave. Will Duncan escape or will he be eaten by a vampire with hideous breath and no ears? (*To PETER:*) I like to leave the endings to him.

PETER. Oh that's nice.

KAREN. Then when he wakes up he tells what happened. It's kind of our party piece.

PETER. I don't believe this.

KAREN. It's true.

PETER. No this! Him, you, your marriage. You can't be serious about this guy!

KAREN. Peter! I love him. Duncan's very sweet, considerate and charming.

PETER. When he's awake.

KAREN. Which he is . . . some of the time.

PETER. Karen, he's fucking Rip Van Winkle.

KAREN. I'm not going to sit here and . . .

PETER. What was it, forty years? That's a lot of nights out bowling, Karen.

KAREN. One more word, Peter. One more word and I'm leaving! I swear!! Change of topic. No better. Let's just shut up for a minute. I'm timing. (*LAUREL Enters with drinks.*)

LAUREL. Bourbon and soda. And the wine for two comes with a complimentary loaf of bread. You want to order now? (*pause*) Is this thing contagious or what? (*LAUREL walks away, but spies on them from a doorway as PETER says in sign language, "Sometimes you drive me crazy."*)

KAREN. That's the same as talking. (*PETER repeats signs.*) What are you trying to say?

PETER. (*As HE signs*) Sometimes . . . you . . . drive . . . me . . . crazy!

LAUREL. "Children of a Lesser God"!!! Am I right?

PETER. We're not ready to order yet!!!

LAUREL. WELL OK!! BUT MAYBE THEY DIDN'T HEAR YOU IN THE KITCHEN!!!!! (*LAUREL Exits.*)

PETER. Look Karen. Before that maniac comes back or Sleeping Beauty wakes up, would you mind telling me one thing, please? (*The following in one breath:*) Would you tell me why, after more than a year, you tracked me down and invited me here? I mean, I really want to know this 'cause you say you love him but then you want to see me which I don't quite understand 'cause I don't want to see you if you're seeing him 'cause I still feel strongly about you and would like you to return these feelings which you say you won't, so I don't want to see you if you won't and you won't so we won't!! So why am I here? (*breath*) I'm leaving, OK. Good-bye.

KAREN. All right, Peter. Sit down. I'll tell you why I called, but first you've got to promise you won't laugh.

PETER. I won't laugh.

KAREN. All right. Two months ago my parents died.

PETER. Jesus. I'm sorry.

KAREN. It's not just that. It's this weird string of events that's happening to me, and I just want it to stop. I mean, first you walk out on me after five years . . .

PETER. Well, after you asked me to leave!

KAREN. That's not how I remember it. And then my folks pass away. And it's weird, but all of a sudden everybody who knew me growing up, everybody who knew me as a kid, as a teen, they're all gone. And it's like, sure I remember my past, but there's nobody around to ask if this really happened or am I dreaming that up. You know? It's like, these people are disappearing and part of me is too. And then Duncan. God bless him. I love him. But every time we get close, it's lights out. And so I get left alone again. And I'm starting to get a little lonely, you know.

PETER. Well I've been pretty lonely, too. (*As PETER reaches for KAREN's hand, DUNCAN wakes up with a start.*)

DUNCAN. Get your hands off her.

PETER. What?

KAREN. Honey . . .

DUNCAN. (*grabbing PETER, then recoiling*) Ahhh, that breath!!!

KAREN. Duncan . . .

DUNCAN. Back!!! I'm gonna rip those ears right off again!! (*DUNCAN grabs PETER in a headlock.*)

PETER. Just a min . . . chgl-chgl-chgl . . .

KAREN. Let him go.

DUNCAN. Get away, god damn it! This is gonna get bloody! (*DUNCAN grabs a knife off the table.*)

KAREN. Duncan stop!!

PETER. Hey! . . . crf-crf-crf . . .

DUNCAN. God damn it, hold still.

KAREN. Listen to me! He's not the vampire in your dreams!!!

DUNCAN. Huh? He's not?

KAREN. No. Let him go. (*DUNCAN drops PETER suddenly.*) That's right. You're awake now.

DUNCAN. I'm what? What's that music?

KAREN. Just an opera.

DUNCAN. (*sees audience*) Who are they? Oh my God. I'm on stage. In an opera! (*He tries to sing, but as in a nightmare, can't.*) My voice! My voice!!! (*For first time the taped opera music has stopped.*)

KAREN. No, honey. You're still dreaming. (*DUNCAN checks out audience.*) Please. It's just a restaurant. You're awake.

DUNCAN. I'm awake. I'm awake!. . . . Thank God.

(*Opera music comes back on.*)

KAREN. And this is Peter. We were about to have dinner.

DUNCAN. Oh yeah. Oh shit, sorry man!

PETER. It's all right.

KAREN. It's my fault honey. I told you that dream. But it's over now. Everything's all right.

DUNCAN. No it's not. No it's not all right, god damn it! I've made an ass of myself again. And you want to know what the irony is, Peter? (*DUNCAN still has knife and waves it wildly.*) You want to know what it is?!?

PETER. OK. Sure.

DUNCAN. They've diagnosed me as a narcoleptic, right? And prescribed medicine to keep me from falling asleep? But when I take the medicine guess what the side effect is. I get sleepy! SLEEPY! You get it!!! That's irony, Peter. Irony!! Ha-ha-ha!! (*laugh turns to tears*)

KAREN. Come on, dear. Just sit down for a minute and rest.

DUNCAN. I don't want to rest. I want No-Doz. I want to marathon dance!

KAREN. (*As DUNCAN hyperventilates, KAREN turns to PETER.*) So, Peter?

PETER. So, Karen?

KAREN. So I'll call you, OK? We can all do a movie or something?

DUNCAN. (*To himself:*) Those damn doctors.

PETER. I don't think that's such a hot idea, Karen.

KAREN. What do you mean?

PETER. I mean, I can't be what you want me to be. I can't be your friend!

KAREN. Why not?

PETER. (*A whispered scream:*) Because I love you!!!!

KAREN. That doesn't make any sense, Peter. We can't be friends because you love me?

PETER. That's right! (*LAUREL Enters.*)

DUNCAN. (*To himself again:*) God why me? Why me?!?

LAUREL. Why not you?

KAREN. (*To PETER:*) Five years is a long time to just throw away. (*To DUNCAN:*) Come on dear. Let's get you home.

DUNCAN. Please don't make me go to bed.

KAREN. I won't, dear. Come on.

DUNCAN. You're the only thing, Karen, that's any good in my life. And I'm gonna love you forever. I promise.

KAREN. I know, honey. I know. (*KAREN and DUNCAN Exit.*)

LAUREL. I give 'em six months, tops. Did you ever think you were in love?

PETER. Once.

LAUREL. Me, too. Now I got a dog. He's clean, he's cheap, and he's always happy to see me. (*Hearing "Pagliacci" aria again:*) Oh, that opera you asked about. That's "Pagliacci," about some creep who goes berzerko and snuffs his wife and her boyfriend.

PETER. Jeez.

LAUREL. A real up, huh? But that's opera for you.

PETER. (*toasting:*) To opera. (*He drains glass.*)

LAUREL. Can I get you anything else—or just the bill?

PETER. You said something earlier about flaming drinks.

LAUREL. That's our specialty.

PETER. You have anything that resembles a blow torch?

LAUREL. We've got one with ten liquors in it.

PETER. What do you call it?

LAUREL. The eternal flame.

PETER. Perfect.

(*LAUREL Exits. As aria from "Pagliacci" comes on again and increases to full volume, PETER takes out a match, lights it, studies the flame, and then puts the match in his mouth, closing his lips around it. After a moment . . .*)

PETER. Owwwww-shit! (*As he reaches for the glass of water the lights fade out.*)

FADE TO BLACK

THE END

The Road to Ruin

by
Richard Dresser

THE ROAD TO RUIN

by

Richard Dresser

1st Production May 26, 1987

Director. . . . . Bob Krakower
Sets. . . . . .Paul Owen
Lights. . . . . Cliff Berek
Costumes. . . . . .Kevin McLeod

CAST

CLIFF. . . . . KEVIN FABIAN
CONNIE. . . . . .JUDY SCHEER
FRED. . . . . REID DAVIS
JIMBO. . . . . NICK PHELPS

CHARACTERS

CLIFF, a man in his thirties
CONNIE, his wife
FRED, a middle-aged auto mechanic
JIMBO, the proprietor of a Jersey City garage

SETTING

The middle of a rainy night at Jimbo's garage. It's in a particularly menacing neighborhood in Jersey City just off the highway. We can see the office of the garage and a small part of the parking lot.

All programs and printed material for this play must carry the following notice:

COMMISSIONED AND FIRST PRODUCED BY ACTORS THEATRE OF LOUISVILLE

The Road to Ruin

AT RISE: Darkness. The sound of rain, then two car doors open, a dog barks, and the car doors slam shut. We hear CLIFF and CONNIE's voices in the lot outside the garage.

CONNIE. I will never ride in that car again.

CLIFF. Then how do you plan to get home?

CONNIE. That's a very good question. Since nobody seems to be here.

CLIFF. Maybe I'll take a quick look at it myself.

CONNIE. You can't even get the hood up, I've seen you try!

CLIFF. That was one time, before they showed me where the little catch is.

CONNIE. We've had the car for two years and you can't get the hood up.

CLIFF. Well if I got just a little bit of support from you it might be different. Come on.

(CLIFF opens the door to the office of JIMBO'S garage. It's illuminated by a fluorescent clock on the wall, a Coke machine, and a neon sign. CONNIE follows CLIFF in out of the rain. They stand in the ghostly light of the office. It contains a desk with a telephone, a wall-phone, and horrible clutter. Besides the doorway leading outside, there's a closed door leading into the garage.)

CONNIE. This place better be open.

CLIFF. *(calling out)* Hello? Anybody here? *(CONNIE sits down. She gets out a small mirror and checks herself out. The door to the garage opens, revealing a blinding white light. FRED Enters. He is covered with grease. He closes the door, switches on the lights in the office, and sits down at the desk, opens the desk drawer, and takes out a sandwich. He eats the sandwich, paying no attention to them. CONNIE looks at CLIFF, challenging him to take charge of the situation. CLIFF tentatively approaches the desk.)* Excuse me, sir. We've got a little problem with our car. We were hoping that you could perhaps take a look at it.

FRED. Can't you see I'm on my break?

CLIFF. Oh, right. Sorry. *(CLIFF crosses to where CONNIE is impatiently sitting. A low voice:)* He's on his break.

CONNIE. (*pained*) For how long?

CLIFF. (*clearing his throat*) Uh, how long would the break be? (*They both watch FRED, but there's no response.*)

CONNIE. Maybe he could give us the key to the ladies room.

CLIFF. Yes, uh, sir? Is there a ladies room key? For my wife?

(*Without turning to them, FRED points toward the corner. They follow where he is pointing. CONNIE goes to the corner and gets a cinder block with the ladies room key on it.*)

CONNIE. Is this it? (*FRED suddenly puts the sandwich back in the drawer and slams it shut.*)

FRED. People steal, okay? (*CONNIE picks up the cinder block and starts outside where FRED is pointing.*)

CONNIE. (*To CLIFF:*) Would you call Triple A? We haven't got all night and he obviously won't help us. (*CONNIE struggles out with the cinder block. CLIFF takes a quarter from his pocket and goes to the wall-phone.*)

CLIFF. Mind if I . . . (*FRED is intently reading a magazine. CLIFF checks the yellow pages, and dials. As he does this, FRED slowly swivels around in his chair and takes CLIFF's wallet from his back pocket. Then he swivels back into his previous position as CLIFF finishes dialing. CLIFF moves toward the doorway, trying to have some privacy from FRED. The phone on FRED's desk rings. FRED answers it. On phone:*) Yes, is this the Automobile Club?

FRED. (*on phone:*) Uh-huh.

CLIFF. I wonder if you can help me. I'm at a station in Jersey City called Jimbo's and my car is broken down. No one here will help us, and I need to get my car towed. It's very important that I get back to the city because my wife has a job interview tomorrow.

FRED. (*on phone:*) What seems to be the problem?

CLIFF. (*on phone:*) It was going and then it stopped . . . (*He turns around and sees FRED on the phone. CLIFF hangs up the phone. FRED hangs up the phone.*) Why are you talking to me?

FRED. You called. I answered.

CLIFF. Why did it ring here?

FRED. This is the only phone you can call from there. Dial any number and it will ring here. Wanna try again?

CLIFF. Will you fix my car?

FRED. What's wrong with it?

CLIFF. It was running fine and then it started making this

sound, like . . . somewhere between a rattle and . . . a
. . . moan . . . and then it stopped and we were lucky enough
to coast down the ramp and right in here.

FRED. Damn lucky.

CLIFF. We thought you could, what is it — give it a jump start
or something.

FRED. It was moaning?

CLIFF. Could you at least look at it?

FRED. Not 'til Jimbo gets here.

CLIFF. You couldn't look at it without him? (*FRED opens
another desk drawer and gets out a cup of coffee. He stares at
CLIFF. Then he gets out a contract from the desk drawer.*)

FRED. Work order. Sign on the X.

(*CLIFF signs. FRED immediately takes a stamp and loudly
bangs it down on the contract in several places. Then he tears
out the bottom sheet and files it in a file cabinet, puts another
in an envelope, stamps the envelope and sends it down a mail
slot. He gives another to CLIFF, who puts it in his pocket
without looking at it. CONNIE Enters from the garage carrying the cinder block, which she drops in the corner.*)

CLIFF. Was it okay? (*No response.*) I mean the bathroom,
sometimes in a place like this . . . but of course maybe they do
keep it clean. You never know.

CONNIE. Did he look at the car?

CLIFF. He hasn't actually looked at it, no, but we discussed it.

CONNIE. And?

CLIFF. He can't look at it until the boss shows up.

CONNIE. Why not?

CLIFF. You know union or insurance or something. There
must be a good reason.

CONNIE. I want to get my dog and my luggage and go home.
(*beat*) When is the boss showing up? (*louder:*) When is he showing
up?

FRED. (*swiveling in the chair to face her*) You won't be talking
so loud. You'll keep your voice down when he shows up.

CLIFF. My wife is a broadcast journalist. She is one of three
candidates to be the week-end weather girl on channel 7. So you
had better show a little goddam respect when addressing her, my
man. (*Headlights outside. FRED immediately puts the coffee cup
back in the drawer and hides the magazine he was reading.*)

CLIFF. Good. Maybe now we can get a little service here. (*JIMBO Enters. He's soaking wet.*)

FRED. (*very politely:*) How is it out there? (*JIMBO glares at FRED, then turns his attention to CLIFF and CONNIE.*)

JIMBO. Whose car is blocking my driveway?

CLIFF. That's our car. It stalled out and we just coasted in here. We thought maybe we could get help, but no one has lifted a finger. (*JIMBO goes menacingly over to FRED, who cowers.*)

JIMBO. Any telephone calls? (*JIMBO and FRED burst into hysterical laughter.*)

CLIFF. Could it be the spark plugs? I hear that if they get wet it can stall a car.

FRED. (*To JIMBO:*) Don't listen to him. He don't know much. (*confidentially:*) She was moaning before she stopped.

CLIFF. Moaning is not what I meant!

JIMBO. (*turning on CLIFF*) I know what's wrong with your car.

CLIFF. Really? (*beat*) What?

JIMBO. Your car is depressed.

CLIFF. That's not possible.

JIMBO. No? (*To FRED:*) He says it's not possible. (*JIMBO opens the door to the garage and Exits into the white light.*)

CONNIE. Did you call the auto club?

CLIFF. I tried.

CONNIE. Good lord. I'm going to call a cab. I have to start putting on my make-up in . . . two hours. (*CONNIE goes to the phone.*)

CLIFF. Don't bother. All the calls go through the desk and he stops them. (*CONNIE dials and the phone rings on the desk. CONNIE hangs up the wall-phone and the phone on the desk stops. FRED smiles at her.*)

CONNIE. We never should have come to New Jersey.

FRED. You people think a car can't get depressed? Take a peek out back. The whole lot is full of 'em. Just sittin' there. They gave up.

CLIFF. (*staring out the window*) What do you do with them?

FRED. Talk to 'em. Try to build up their self-esteem. (*JIMBO comes back in. FRED spins around in his chair and studies the papers on his desk.*)

JIMBO. That was a helluva place to leave your car.

CONNIE. We didn't mean to leave it there—

CLIFF. That's where it happened to stop. Believe me, there was absolutely no planning on our part.

JIMBO. (*To FRED:*) Move it.

FRED. We got no room —

JIMBO. Make room! (*FRED jumps up and goes outside.*)

CLIFF. I signed a work order and I'm going to insist that you live up to it.

JIMBO. He got you to sign?

CLIFF. It's right here. I'm a man who respects a contract. (*beat*) How soon can you look at my car?

JIMBO. Depends.

CLIFF. On what?

JIMBO. On how bad it is.

CLIFF. How can you tell how bad it is if you don't look?

JIMBO. You're a wise-guy, aren't you? I could put your nose in a lug wrench. Give it a couple of turns and then we'd see how wise you are.

CLIFF. My wife has to put on her cosmetics. If you can't look at the car tonight, then we'll have to leave it here.

JIMBO. I'm all backed up. No way will your car stay here tonight.

CONNIE. Maybe you'd like to buy it.

CLIFF. Connie!

CONNIE. (*urgent whisper:*) It's a perfect chance to get rid of it!

JIMBO. I don't buy'em anymore. Too much trouble.

CLIFF. Then what will it cost for you to look at it right now? Fifty bucks?

JIMBO. Put'er on the table. (*CLIFF reaches for his wallet, which is gone.*)

CLIFF. My God, Connie. My wallet —

CONNIE. What?

CLIFF. It's gone —

CONNIE. And I didn't bring my purse —

CLIFF. (*To JIMBO:*) Listen, we seem to have misplaced our money. But we've got every credit card you can name. We have a mortgage, bank cards, securities, mutual funds, IRAs, you name it. We're good for the money.

JIMBO. People like you I see by the hundreds. They never pay up.

CLIFF. Don't judge me by the others! I'll give you my watch! (*CLIFF puts his watch on the desk.*)

CONNIE. Cliff, we can't even take the train if we don't have money.

JIMBO. Let me tell you a story. One of 'em came in here, he

could have been your twin. Tried to give me a *personal check.*
(*Pause. CLIFF and CONNIE aren't sure if the story is over.*)

CLIFF. What happened?

JIMBO. He turned out to be a bad credit risk. (*JIMBO presses a buzzer on the desk and makes a violent motion out the window. There is a loud, grating sound.*)

CLIFF. Your jewelry, Connie—

CONNIE. Cliff! (*CONNIE starts taking off her jewelry and putting it on the desk.*)

CLIFF. All of it, Connie! (*CONNIE moans and takes off more. JIMBO slides it into the desk drawer, which he closes.*)

CLIFF. And if that isn't enough, then we'll give him Ramon—

CONNIE. Not Ramon!

CLIFF. (*To JIMBO:*) She's got a dog in the car that's worth six grand. He just won every prize at the show, for Chrissakes this dog could do your taxes if you want. He's yours. You can barbecue the sucker for all I care. I just want you to know that we are people who are as good as our word—

CONNIE. We are not going to give this man Ramon!

CLIFF. Listen to reason, Connie. We are going to give him whatever he wants. We have no car and no money—

(*FRED comes in pushing a little hand truck with a cube of compressed metal on it.*)

JIMBO. I've changed my mind. You can leave your car here now because we have the room.

FRED. Where do you want it, boss?

CONNIE. (*a small, stricken voice:*) That's our car, isn't it?

CLIFF. What have you done?

CONNIE. My God. Ramon! Where is Ramon? (*To FRED:*) Was there a dog in there?

FRED. (*To the metal block:*) Here boy! Here boy! (*To CONNIE:*) He don't come when you call.

JIMBO. Put'er way in back. They're last in line and they got no money.

CLIFF. I loved that car! (*turning on JIMBO*) How could you do that?

JIMBO. (*turning to FRED*) You can get cleaned up, Fred. (*FRED wheels the hand-truck into the garage.*)

JIMBO. (*To CLIFF:*) See? Take away your money and you're just like everybody else.

CONNIE. Come on, Cliff. We'll walk.

JIMBO. I give you two blocks, maybe three. Then they'll get you.

CONNIE. Nobody's going to "get us."

JIMBO. A healthy pair like you? You get picked up and bought and sold and bought and sold and pretty soon you're on the other side of the world bent over in the hot sun harvesting cocoa plants. (*beat*) The only way to leave this place is in a car. And you ain't got one.

CLIFF. Okay. We'll wait here—

JIMBO. You wait here you gotta work. That way you'll be able to get another car.

CLIFF. Okay, we'll work tonight. I don't mind.

JIMBO. What can you do? Can you fix things? (*beat*) 'Course not. Professionals. Can't do a damn thing and I got three acres of cars turning into scrap iron.

CLIFF. I could talk to the cars . . . try to cheer 'em up.

CONNIE. God, Cliff.

JIMBO. Fair enough. And maybe some day one of 'em will be yours. (*beat*) 'Course I gotta charge you rent.

CLIFF. Fine. Take it out of my pay. (*beat*) How much do I get?

JIMBO. It's all in the contract you signed.

CLIFF. What contract? (*CLIFF looks blank. Then he hurriedly gets out the paper he signed.*) My God. I thought it was a work order. I'll never get away . . . Connie . . .

JIMBO. It's already gone to the central office. Try to break a contract with *them* . . .

(*FRED Enters, wearing Bermuda shorts, sun-glasses, and sandals with high black socks. He's carrying a work shirt, which he tosses on the chair. He stops at the desk and puts on CLIFF's watch. FRED takes out his wallet—which is CLIFF's wallet—and carefully counts out some bills, which he gives to JIMBO.*)

FRED. That's the last of it. I'd say we're square, boss.

JIMBO. (*looks at his watch*) Your shift is done, Fred. (*beat*) Seven years to the day. Now you got your choice of cars. (*FRED goes to the wall where a number of keys are hanging. He selects one.*)

FRED. (*To CLIFF:*) The pay's okay but the rent's worse. (*FRED starts for the door.*)

CLIFF. You're leaving?

FRED. I done my time.

CONNIE. Could you give us a ride? Oh, please, just get us across the bridge—

JIMBO. Not this one. He works here now.

CONNIE. Then take me, please, Manhattan's right over there—

CLIFF. Connie!

FRED. I guess I could do that.

CLIFF. What about me?

JIMBO. You signed up to have your car fixed—

CLIFF. How can you fix it now?

JIMBO. It'll take time. Gotta send out for parts. And there's a whole slew of people in front of you. You'll meet 'em, living in their cars, wandering through the lot out back. Nice folks who ran into some car trouble. You gotta wait your turn, just like everyone else.

CONNIE. I'll come back for you, Cliff. As soon as I get the job—

FRED. That's what they all say. (*beat*) I was coming through here with the wife and kids. A week's holiday at the shore, you know? We get off the highway to look for a place to eat. The car stalls, right out front. We thought we were lucky, a garage right handy. Jimbo put the car out back with the others. We kept waiting for it to get better, but it never did. Months go by, I'm pumping gas, we're living in the car wash. This wasn't much of a place for the kids to grow up, so one morning the wife says she's gonna take the kids and make a break for it, try to get out and get help. That was six and a half years ago. Some vacation.

CONNIE. Cliff, you know I'd stay if it weren't for the job.

CLIFF. I know, darling. (*beat*) Maybe I'll see you on TV.

CONNIE. I sure hope so, Cliff. (*They embrace. Then CONNIE and FRED leave. CLIFF watches them.*)

JIMBO. The sooner you start the sooner you can leave. That's just common sense.

(*CLIFF takes off his shirt and puts on the work shirt that FRED brought out. It fits perfectly, and has CLIFF's name over the pocket. CLIFF opens the door to the garage and steps into the white light. Blackout.*)

THE END

The Drummer

by

Athol Fugard

THE DRUMMER by Athol Fugard

1st production February 27, 1980
Director. . . . . Michael Hankins
Sets. . . . . .Paul Owen
Lights. . . . . Jeff Hill
Costumes. . . . . .Kurt Wilhelm

CAST

The MAN. . . . . DIERK TOPORZYSEK

SETTING

A city pavement.

All programs and printed materials for this play must carry the
following notice:

COMMISSIONED AND FIRST PRODUCED BY ACTORS THEATRE OF LOUISVILLE

The Drummer

SCENE: A pile of rubbish on a pavement, waiting to be cleared away. This consists of an over-filled trash-can and a battered old chair with torn upholstery on which is piled an assortment of cardboard boxes and plastic bags full of discarded junk. Distant and intermittent city noises. These will increase in volume and frequency as the action demands.

(AT RISE: A BUM Enters. He walks over to the pile of rubbish and starts to work his way through it . . . looking for something useful in terms of that day's survival. He has obviously just woken up and yawns from time to time. After a few seconds he clears the chair, sits down, makes himself comfortable and continues his search. One of the boxes produces a drumstick. He examines it and then abandons it. A little later he finds a second drumstick. He examines it. Remembers! He scratches around in the pile of rubbish at his feet and retrieves the first. Two drumsticks! His find intrigues him. Another dip into the rubbish but it produces nothing further of interest. Two drumsticks! He settles back in his chair and surveys the world.
An ambulance siren approaches and recedes stage right. He observes indifferently. A fire engine approaches and recedes stage left. He observes. While this is going on he taps idly on the lid of the trash-can with one of the drumsticks. He becomes aware of this little action. Two drumsticks and a trash-can! It takes him a few seconds to realize the potential. He straightens up in his chair and with a measure of caution, attempts a little tattoo on the lid of the can. The result is not very impressive. He makes a second attempt, with the same result. Problem. Solution! He gets up and empties the trash-can of its contents, replaces the lid and makes a third attempt. The combination of a serious intention and the now resonant bin produces a decided affect. He develops it and in doing so starts to enjoy himself. His excitement gets him onto his feet. He has one last flash of inspiration. He removes the lid from the can, up-ends it, and with great bravuro drums out a final tattoo . . . virtually an accompaniment to the now very loud and urgent city noises all around him. Embellishing his appearance with some item from the rubbish . . . a cape? . . . and holding his drumsticks ready he chooses a

direction and sets off to take on the city. He has discovered it is full of drums . . . and he has got drumsticks.

THE BEGINNING

Perfect

by
Mary Gallagher

PERFECT by Mary Gallagher

1st Production May 28, 1985

Director. . . . . Kenneth Washington
Sets. . . . . .Paul Owen
Lights. . . . . Janine Silver
Costumes. . . . . Ellen A. MacAvoy

CAST

Tina. .MARGARET TERRANOVA
Kitty. . . . . KELLY McBRIDE
Dan. . . . . RYAN REID

SETTING

A house or an apartment.

TIME

The Present

All programs and publicity material for this play must carry the following notice:

COMMISSIONED AND FIRST PRODUCED BY ACTORS THEATRE OF LOUISVILLE

Perfect

SCENE: *A house or an apartment, with a hallway, pantry, or other in-between, in-transit space. A counter, table or hamper for people to perch or lean on.*

AT RISE: *There is a small dinner party going on. TINA and KITTY Enter, TINA intercepting KITTY, demanding as she stops her:*

TINA. So wadaya think?

KITTY. So far, he's fine —

TINA. So far?! I think he is perfect!

KITTY. He's great-looking, that's for sure —

TINA. And *smart,* God, he's like Joe Genius at the law firm, Binky says —

KITTY. He seems like he's bright, he's read a book lately, at least —

TINA. He reads like a maniac. Like at *lunch.* Binky says everybody else goes out and gets loaded with the clients and here's Dan still at the old desk with the p.b. sandwiches and the *book* —

KITTY. He's got a sense of humor too. I mean I think he's said a lot of funny things tonight. Witty. Perceptive, even —

TINA. *(overlapping)* Are you kidding? God, he is *hysterical*! He gets Binks laughing on the phone, like Binks can't stop, like with *tears* —

KITTY. And he offered to help clear the table. (*TINA's jaw drops. She is speechless.*) I know.

TINA. Because they *don't,* you know. *Still.* They *won't.*

KITTY. *(nods)* It's like the last bastion. The Alamo.

TINA. Yeah. They like . . . dig in, they get this *rigid* look . . .

KITTY. Sort of daunted, but *entrenched* —

TINA. And they start talking sports.

KITTY. Or business-man-talk. "To the best of my knowledge, Fred."

TINA. Right! Right! That's the best thing about Binky being Binky. When people start that crap with him, it just doesn't cut it. "To the best of my knowledge, Binky." (*They start giggling. They lean on each other, giggling. DAN Enters.*)

DAN. You guys are having a good time in here. Binks and I are missing it. We feel ripped off. We feel we should express that.

KITTY. And we're glad you did. (*He keeps looking at her for a beat. There is clearly a strong mutual attraction. They are faintly smiling. TINA enjoys this. Then:*)

DAN. Well, troops. Binky sent me to inquire, I quote, "What is the coffee situation?"

TINA. It's working, tell him. He's the one that bought a Chemex, tell him. So he can learn to wait. What's he think this is, the Dog n' Suds?

DAN. How 'bout if I tell him it's almost ready?

KITTY. Tell him, "Almost ready, to the best of my knowledge, Binky."

DAN. (*grins*) "This is just an estimate, based on available data, Binks." (*goes out*)

TINA. (*poking KITTY, referring to the vibes*) WOO!

KITTY. Yeah. It's great. So far.

TINA. What is this "So far?!" There is no hidden horror. Trust me, I *told* you, I looked *into* him, not only is he not attached, he has the perfect history! He was married, once, so he isn't afraid of commitment, but they were very young, and it just didn't work. No kids. Plus his ex-wife has a great job so he pays no alimony, and he even plays squash with her, so he's not bitter. *But*, they've been divorced for five years and he's dated a *lot* and *lived* with at least one other woman, maybe two, so we know he's not hung up on her. Plus he's stayed friends with the *other* women. *Plus*, he has two nephews and a niece and he adores them, takes them everywhere, so he's not *opposed* to kids. He drinks like just enough, he gets loose but not sloppy, and he'll smoke some dope if someone passes it around but he never turns into an asshole. I mean, if you don't take him, take Binky and *I'll* take him!

KITTY. I really am attracted to him. I mean he turns me on, I can't—

TINA. Tell me about it! I can see it! It's like . . . a force!

KITTY. Yeah?

TINA. *Yeah*! . . . Also you keep grinning.

KITTY. I do? Oh, God—

TINA. You *both* do. Me and Binky feel left out.

KITTY. God, how embarrassing—

TINA. So what's the hold-up?

KITTY. . . . You're gonna get pissed off.

TINA. I might, I'll tell ya. I oughta get anointed queen for coming up with him. Or Pope! 'Cause do you know what's *out there*?

KITTY. I know, I know, believe me . . . Okay. It's this. I'm just afraid . . . okay, look at the evidence. He's a lawyer. He makes a lot of money—

TINA. It's not that great. He makes like what Binky makes, it isn't—

KITTY. Compared to say the average income of the average working—

TINA. Okay, okay, right—

KITTY. He plays squash. He drives an Audi. He went to Fiji for a month last year. He probably *invests*. He's what? Twenty-seven?

TINA. Twenty-eight. That's better, men are assholes till they're twenty-eight. See? He's even twenty-eight! *What are you afraid of?*

KITTY. Who do you think he voted for?

TINA. (*Stopped; then, stalling for time:*) Huh?

KITTY. That's what I figured. *Shit.*

TINA. Wait a minute, wait a minute—

KITTY. God, it's all so depressing—

TINA. *Wait* a minute, we don't know—

KITTY. You know. You know in your heart—

TINA. I don't! You *never* know! Binky's just the same as Dan, he's practically a clone of Dan, and Binky didn't vote for him!

KITTY. Only because the last time, you told Binky if he voted for him, he would not get laid for four more years—

TINA. But he might not have voted for him anyway. Binky *adored* Ferraro, he wanted to sleep with her, he even tried for her sake to believe her husband wasn't guilty! And Binky, I mean Binky *knew*, his law career is *based* on crooked real estate—

KITTY. I don't care how Binky voted! It's how Dan voted!

TINA. Well. I don't think it's fair. For you to just . . . assume . . .

KITTY. I bet Binky knows.

TINA. (*stalling:*) I don't think they talk politics.

KITTY. I'm gonna ask him.

TINA. Why don't you just ask Dan? Go ahead! Just . . . ! (*Throws up hands.*)

KITTY. (*bleakly*) 'Cause if he did vote for him, I'd cry . . . or puke, or something . . . (*Trails off. Pause. Then:*)

TINA. (*gently*) Look. Why don't you wait. You know? See how it goes. Enjoy it for a while. You've really hit it off. You could have so much fun. God, he could be the greatest lover in America! Why ruin it before you even—?

KITTY. No. I like him too much already. I just can't face getting suckered in, but at the same time worrying, suspecting . . . and finally *finding out*! I'd rather end it now. One clean . . . (*Guillotine gesture sweeping down; continues:*) We'll go back in, I'll ask him.

TINA. Now, God damn it! This is really foolish. This is self-destructive. I don't think you *want* to have a good relationship. Or even a good *time*. I think . . . I think, and I'm serious, you are *avoiding* having a relationship with a healthy man—

KITTY. There are certain things . . . beliefs, principles . . . gut instincts, call it what you will . . . that every person has to cling to. And they're different for every person. That's what makes us who we are. I would not ask *you* to give up the deep convictions that you have . . .

TINA. (*annoyed*) Name one!

KITTY. . . . and you would not want *me* to throw away my deepest, most dearly-held—

TINA. I want you to have a nice man in your life! I want you to be happy!

KITTY. . . . Yeah, I know. And I appreciate it. And I want that too. I do. But I can't stand the way the world is going! And if I can't stop it, at least I won't participate! I won't sleep with anyone who voted for him!

TINA. (*Beat; then, flatly:*) You're talking about everybody. Everybody voted for him—

KITTY. No! Not everybody! Last time, forty-one per cent voted for Walter Mondale! You know how many people that is? Forty-one per cent of all the people in the entire United States, who voted, voted for Walter Mondale! Not to mention all the people who were too disheartened, too broken in spirit by four hellish years of Ronald Reagan—

TINA. Oh God, here we go—

KITTY. —or too weak and wasted, *drained*, from four long years of *rage* . . . to drag their bodies to the polls . . . those people did not vote for him! People who can't bear to vote do not constitute a mandate—!

TINA. Look, do me a favor, please, don't ask him tonight. I don't need a bloodbath here.

KITTY. Oh great, let's all pretend this isn't happening—

TINA. I don't like him either. But you are not rational about this—

KITTY. People who were rational put an *actor* in the White House! Who *is* that guy? *He* doesn't know! One minute he thinks he's playing FDR, he's looking for his wheelchair, then he's doing Lionel Barrymore in "Calling Dr. Kildare," he's at a summit meeting and he's looking for Lew Ayres! Then he starts the intro to the General Electric show, he's saying, "You know, Gorby, progress is our most important product" — (*DAN Enters. They look at each other. TINA watches, grins. Then:*)

TINA. I think the coffee's ready. (*TINA Exits. DAN and KITTY look at each other: same strong attraction. Slight smiles begin. Silence. Then:*)

DAN. Want to have dinner tomorrow night?

KITTY. (*Hovers on the brink, then:*) Did you vote for Reagan?

DAN. (*surprised:*) Actually, I didn't vote in '84. Terrible, I know. But I got packed off to Kuwait by the firm, with two days notice, and I didn't have time to do the absentee ballot routine.

KITTY. Oh . . . huh. (*Even more torn: can she let this be a reprieve? Greatly tempted:*) I . . . I *would* like to have dinner . . .

DAN. Great.

KITTY. I'd *really* like to sleep with you.

DAN. (*Thrown, but:*) Terrific. (*They move as one into their first embrace. Just before the kiss:*)

KITTY. (*Can't help herself:*) If you *had* voted, who would you have —

BLACKOUT

THE END

Loyalties

by
Murphy Guyer

LOYALTIES by Murphy Guyer

1st Production December 17, 1984

Director. . . . . Robert Spera
Sets. . . . . Laura Luisa Cowell
Lights. . . . . Geoff Korf
Costumes. . . . . Hollis Jenkins-Evans

CAST

RUDY. . . . . DOUG WERT
KATRIN. . . . . CORNELIA EVANS
MONIKA. . . . . RAYE LANKFORD
JACOB. . . . . LOUIS DiVINCENTI

SETTING

A dining room.

All programs and printed material for this play must carry the
following notice:

COMMISSIONED AND FIRST PRODUCED BY ACTORS
THEATRE OF LOUISVILLE

Loyalties

SCENE: *A round table with four chairs. Solid oak. A white linen tablecloth. In the center of the table sits a half consumed chocolate cake. Also, two bottles of champagne. One empty, the other half full. There are four settings at the table. Each with a glass of champagne and a plate stained with the remains of chocolate cake. Four crumpled linen napkins. Upstage left is a large wooden door.*

AT RISE: *We see MONIKA, JACOB, KATRIN, and RUDY seated at the table. MONIKA and KATRIN are both wearing dresses of simple cut and style. They evoke no particular period or fashion. JACOB is wearing a plain black suit, worn and bohemian. He wears a white shirt. No tie. RUDY wears the brown pants of a military uniform, with a matching brown t-shirt. Brown socks and no boots.*

RUDY. He's done a remarkable job, no doubt about it. Thanks to him this country is back on it's feet again . . . Where's the cake knife?

MONIKA. Here, hon.

RUDY. People are starting to act like citizens again. They're starting to care about more then just making it through the next day.

KATRIN. That was because of inflation.

RUDY. Sure it was. Hell, I'm not blaming them. They had no choice. Anybody else for more cake? (*To MONIKA:*) Birthday girl?

MONIKA. Well, maybe just a little. Not too much though . . . No Rudy, smaller. Smaller! Rudy! I can't eat all that! What are you doing? Take some of that back. You'll ruin my waistline.

RUDY. To hell with your waistline. You're getting too skinny anyway. I got nothing to hold on to anymore.

MONIKA. Rudy! Not in front of the guests.

RUDY. What guests? It's your sister.

MONIKA. (*giggling*) He's got a one track mind, I swear.

RUDY. (*offering cake*) Katrin?

KATRIN. No more for me, thanks.

RUDY. Jake? Cake? Cake, Jake?

JACOB. No thanks.

RUDY. How's *that* for poetry? What do you think? Think I've got a future?

JACOB. It's Jacob.

RUDY. No good. Can't use it. Doesn't rhyme with cake. Can't be poetry if it doesn't rhyme.

JACOB. Think of it as blank verse.

RUDY. Ha ha. Good one, good one . . . What did I do with my fork?

MONIKA. You dropped it on the floor. I'll get you another one.

RUDY. Forget it. I'll use Jake's. (*He wipes JACOB'S fork off with his napkin.*) Where was I? Oh yeah — no, no, I'm not blaming them. They were scared to death. And why wouldn't they be? Their life savings were being wiped out right in front of their eyes. Millions of people out of work? No, it was a desperate situation, no doubt about it. But what made it really bad was that there wasn't anybody in charge. There wasn't any confidence in the future because there wasn't anybody to inspire it. I mean let's face it, since we lost that goddam war, this country has been in a daze. People suddenly just lost faith in all the traditional values. I mean forget discipline. Forget self sacrifice. It was just me, me, me. Either something had to change or this country wasn't going to make it.

MONIKA. But it *has* changed.

RUDY. That's what I'm saying. That's my point. The whole situation has turned around. Inflation is down, crime is down, the military is strong again, and the communists are running scared. Hell, no wonder the election was such a landslide. For the first time in twenty years, people can finally feel proud of their country again.

MONIKA. Tell them about that woman at the newsstand.

RUDY. I'm getting to that. Will you let me finish? . . . You're not going to eat your cake?

MONIKA. I can't. It's too much I told you.

RUDY. Jesus Christ. Give it to me. . . . Here's a perfect example of what I'm talking about. The other day I went into this newsstand to buy a paper. And there was this old lady there. Must have been about sixty, sixty-five. Didn't look like she had much money. Anyway, from the moment I walked in, all that woman did was stare at me. And I thought to myself, "Oh no, here we go again. She's going to throw a fit."

MONIKA. That happened a couple of weeks ago. This woman

saw Rudy at the train station and started screaming at him. He didn't even do anything. She started screaming. What was it that she called you?

RUDY. I don't know. She was crazy.

MONIKA. It was really filthy.

RUDY. She was nuts. She was like one of those mad dogs that go into convulsions every time a uniform walks by.

JACOB. Did you shoot her?

RUDY. Ha, ha, ha. I should have.

KATRIN. Jacob.

JACOB. Just asking.

KATRIN. Don't start.

RUDY. Oh come on Katrin, he's just joking.

KATRIN. I mean it, Jacob.

MONIKA. What's wrong? What's going on?

KATRIN. Jacob's had too much to drink.

RUDY. Oh hell, Katrin, let the guy enjoy himself. Pay no attention to her, Jake. Eat, drink, and be merry.

JACOB. Thanks, Rude.

RUDY. Ha, ha. Good one, good one.

MONIKA. Come on Rudy, finish your story.

RUDY. Right, right. So anyway I pay for the newspaper and I'm just about to walk out the door when this old lady grabs me by the arm. And I thought to myself, "Here it comes." And you know what she does? She pulls me down and whispers "It makes me proud to see young men in uniform again. God bless you. We could use more like you.". . . .

MONIKA. Isn't that sweet?

RUDY. How about *that*? Now that kind of thing just wasn't happening a few years ago.

MONIKA. And it's true. It does make you feel proud.

RUDY. The woman actually had tears in her eyes.

MONIKA. I love that story.

JACOB. How do you know she wasn't crazy?

KATRIN. Jacob.

RUDY. What?

MONIKA. No, no, that was the other one.

KATRIN. That's enough.

RUDY. Wait a minute, wait a minute. I want to hear what he has to say.

KATRIN. He's drunk. He's just being contrary.

RUDY. What did you mean by that?

JACOB. I just think it's interesting that's all.

MONIKA. What's interesting?

JACOB. That you assume that the woman who berated you was insane while the one who flattered you was perfectly normal.

MONIKA. She was berating him in a public place.

JACOB. He was flattered in a public place.

MONIKA. But she was screaming.

JACOB. The insane never whisper?

RUDY. You're not saying that it's crazy to be patriotic, I hope.

JACOB. I wouldn't call it absolute proof of sanity.

MONIKA. What's wrong with patriotism?

RUDY. Nothing. It's perfectly natural.

JACOB. So is death and disease.

RUDY. And what is that supposed to mean?

JACOB. Just because a thing is natural doesn't make it desirable.

RUDY. If patriotism is anything, it's a cure.

JACOB. It seems to me more like a symptom.

MONIKA. Of what?

JACOB. Of personal weakness.

MONIKA. What's weak about feeling patriotic?

JACOB. To feel patriotic is to feel superior. To celebrate one country is to implicitly denigrate all others. And the feeling of superiority that comes with patriotism is a coward's superiority. It risks nothing. The man who proclaims the greatness of his country is a man who doesn't have the courage to proclaim his own individual greatness.

RUDY. Are you saying that patriots are cowards?

MONIKA. But what about all the men who have died for their country?

JACOB. They did not "die for their country."

RUDY. The hell they didn't!

JACOB. They were killed while trying to kill for their country.

RUDY. Well, however you want to put it, the fact is that they sacrificed their lives for the good of their country!

JACOB. Soldiers do not go into battle with the intention of sacrificing anything. Least of all their lives. And how you *put it*, as you say, means everything. The expression "He died for his country" did not originate with the dying soldier. It was invented by a political eulogist for political purposes. He needed to reassure the grieving parents, and to recruit more young heroes to take the dead soldier's place. It's rhetoric. The manipulation of words for emotional effect to achieve a political purpose.

RUDY. You're the one who's manipulating words for effect.

JACOB. What effect?

RUDY. To win people over to your sick point of view.

JACOB. I don't care whether you agree with my point of view or not. I'm a poet, not a politician. I say what I say because I believe it's true.

MONIKA. But what about the Olympics? Didn't you feel proud when this country won all those medals?

JACOB. Individual athletes won those medals. And their pride is the honest pride of individual effort. The people who appropriate that pride in the name of patriotism are nothing more than chauvinistic cannibals. Their own achievements have so little value they have to confiscate the achievements of their so called "country."

RUDY. The achievements of a country *are* the achievements of its people!

JACOB. The achievements of Mozart are not the achievements of Austria.

RUDY. Mozart is a product of Austria.

JACOB. You make him sound like an industrial export.

RUDY. He was born and raised in Austria.

JACOB. So were millions of others, whose only talent was for giving birth to millions more.

MONIKA. But without Austria there would have been no Mozart.

JACOB. Austria is a political invention, like all countries. It was not created for the purpose of cultivating Mozarts, and so it has no right to claim his genius for its own.

RUDY. So you feel no loyalty to your own country.

JACOB. No.

RUDY. After all this country has given you.

JACOB. I don't see that this country has given me any more than Austria gave to Mozart.

MONIKA. But what about the language? You couldn't write poetry without that.

JACOB. Not everyone who speaks the language is a poet. And not every poet speaks this language.

RUDY. What *do* you feel loyalty towards?

JACOB. My work, my friends.

RUDY. And what about the rest of the world? What about belief in a cause?

JACOB. The world can take care of itself. My only cause is my own mind.

RUDY. It would be a hell of a world if everyone felt the way you did.

JACOB. Almost no one does. They never have and probably never will. And it's still a hell of a world in spite of that.

RUDY. And if your country were suddenly attacked you wouldn't defend it?

JACOB. I'm not a soldier. I'm a poet. I have no interest in fighting. My only interest is to understand the truth as best I can.

RUDY. Yeah, some poet! You've never even been published.

MONIKA. Rudy!

RUDY. Well it's true, isn't it?

KATRIN. Thanks, Monika.

MONIKA. We were talking. It just came up. You didn't say it was supposed to be a secret.

RUDY. I mean if we're only supposed to say things because they're true. . . .

MONIKA. Stop it, Rudy. Don't be spiteful.

RUDY. Who's being spiteful? I just always thought that you had to be published before you could call yourself a poet.

KATRIN. Jacob happens to be a very fine poet.

RUDY. Yeah, well, you seem to be the only one who thinks so.

KATRIN. Everyone will think so someday.

RUDY. And since when did you become such an expert on poetry?

MONIKA. Alright, Rudy, stop it.

RUDY. You probably never even *read* a poem until you met him.

MONIKA. Rudy, stop it. Leave my sister alone.

RUDY. No, no, come on, we're supposed to be telling the truth here, right?

MONIKA. Katrin has been reading books ever since she was a little girl. She's read more than you and me put together.

RUDY. How do you know how many books I've read?!

KATRIN. Look, let's just stop this, alright?

RUDY. I mean, how the hell can somebody just *decide* that he's a poet? If that's all it takes, maybe I'll just decide that I'm a doctor. He doesn't need to publish, and I don't need to take a medical exam! How's that?

MONIKA. Oh be quiet. You're being ignorant.

RUDY. Don't call me that! Don't you ever call me that!

MONIKA. Well, stop picking on everybody.

RUDY. You're supposed to be my wife!

MONIKA. But Katrin's my sister.

RUDY. Well it's time you decided who's side you're on.

MONIKA. But you're not being fair. If Jacob wants to call himself a poet, why can't he? Who cares if he's been published or not? Do you have to kill somebody before you can call yourself a soldier?

RUDY. Hey, I don't care what the hell he calls himself! But I'll be damned if I'm going to sit here and listen to him call patriots cowards.

KATRIN. He never said that.

RUDY. Because let me tell you something, *Jake*! *I'm* patriotic. And so is everybody in my squad. Now are you going to tell me that those men don't have courage?

JACOB. I can't see that it takes much courage to mindlessly march to your own death on someone else's command.

RUDY. Are you saying that soldiers are mindless?!

(*The following exchange accelerates and overlaps.*)

JACOB. You fight when you are ordered to fight. I call that not having a mind of your own.

RUDY. You sonofabitch.

MONIKA. Rudy!

RUDY. I'm defending your freedom, you bastard!

MONIKA. Rudy, stop it!

JACOB. Right . . .

KATRIN. Jacob.

JACOB. . . . as long as I don't exercise it by disagreeing with you.

KATRIN. Jacob! That's enough!

RUDY. You know what you are?

MONIKA. Come on, Rudy!

RUDY. You're a selfish fucking egotist!

MONIKA. You're ruining the party!

JACOB. And you're an interchangeable part.

(*In one rapid movement, RUDY lunges at JACOB, pulls him from the chair, and punches him hard in the belly. JACOB crumples to the floor. The following exchange coincides.*)

MONIKA. Rudy! For godsake!

KATRIN. STOP IT!

MONIKA. Leave him alone! (*KATRIN rushes to JACOB.*)

RUDY. If you hate this country so much, why don't you just leave it?

KATRIN. You stay away from him.

MONIKA. Come on Rudy, stop it, that's enough.

JACOB. I intend to.

RUDY. Yeah, well do us all a favor and make it soon.

KATRIN. Monika! Get him out of here.

JACOB. Will next week be soon enough?

MONIKA. Come on Rudy, you have to get ready. You'll be late.

RUDY. (*As he Exits off right.*) Goddam little fucking traitor.

KATRIN. Bastard!

MONIKA. It's not all his fault!

KATRIN. Who attacked who, Monika?

MONIKA. Well tell Jacob to keep his mouth shut.

KATRIN. Why? He's right?

MONIKA. Rudy is not a coward!

KATRIN. You call what he just did an act of courage?

MONIKA. He was provoked!

KATRIN. Yes. By the truth.

MONIKA. Get out! Get out of our house, both of you! Get out and stay out! I don't care if you are my sister! I won't let you come in here and call my husband a coward! Rudy happens to be one of the bravest men I ever met! (*She exits.*)

KATRIN. Are you alright?

JACOB. Leave me alone.

KATRIN. Well that was childish.

JACOB. It was true.

KATRIN. So what? Did you have to say it?

JACOB. I meant about my leaving next week.

KATRIN. What?

JACOB. I *am* leaving next week.

KATRIN. . . . . For where?

JACOB. Paris.

KATRIN. . . . . For how long?

JACOB. I'm not planning on coming back.

KATRIN. . . . . And what about me?

JACOB. I have nothing to offer you, Katrin. I have no money and I don't see how I could expect to get any anytime soon.

KATRIN. Well, maybe I have my own money. Did you ever think of that?

JACOB. Do you?

KATRIN. . . . . No.

JACOB. I can't support you, Katrin. I can't take that responsibility. It would interfere with my work.

KATRIN. So you have to leave because of your work.

JACOB. Yes.

KATRIN. Well I don't see why. You've been working just fine right here.

JACOB. I haven't been working just fine here. That's why I'm leaving.

KATRIN. And you think you'll be able to work any better in Paris?

JACOB. I can't stay in this country. It's spiritually bankrupt.

KATRIN. And what about me? Am I spiritually bankrupt too?

JACOB. I didn't say that.

KATRIN. No, I'm just an albatross, right?. . . . Right?!

JACOB. I'm sorry.

KATRIN. Fine. Well, I hope you and your work will be very happy together. (*She crosses to the door.*) Rudy was right. You're a selfish sonofabitch.

(*She exits. JACOB remains on the floor. After a moment, RUDY re-enters from* S.R.. *He is now in full uniform. It is a Nazi uniform. He carries his boots. He sees JACOB and stops. They stare at each other for a long moment. JACOB rises and Exits out the door. RUDY sits and drops his boots. MONIKA Enters and goes to clear the table. After a pause, RUDY bursts out emotionally.*)

RUDY. Is it me?! Am I crazy? Am I wrong? Is it wrong to love your country? Is it wrong to be willing to fight for it? I love this country, goddammit! I love it! I know it's not perfect. But what is? I mean you have to believe in something, right? Is it wrong to want to believe in something bigger than yourself? Is it crazy to want to be part of something? To be a part of something that's so much a part of you? Tell me! Is that crazy? Is it me?

KATRIN. No, of course it's not. I love this country too. As much as you do. No Rudy, it's not you. It's not you, honey. It's not.

FADE TO BLACK

THE END

The Asshole Murder Case

by
Stuart Hample

THE ASSHOLE MURDER CASE by Stuart Hample

1st Production February 18, 1981

Director. . . . . Radha Delamarter
Sets. . . . . .Paul Owen
Lights. . . . . Jeff Hill
Costumes. . . . . .Kurt Wilhelm

CAST

NELSON. . . . . .TIMOTHY BUSFIELD
SEYMOUR. . . . . GREG ALEXANDER
EMILY. . . . . .SALLY FAYE REIT
MR. EPSTEIN. . . . . .KENT BROADHURST

CHARACTERS

SEYMOUR — full of rage at authority, feels deep alienation. Uses his humor and Dadaist madness to hide all of this. Wears red knit hat.
NELSON — The opposite of Seymour; he accepts life, indeed, approves of it. Frightened of his feelings; may not even know what they are. (*NELSON & SEYMOUR are room mates, drama majors, and close friends.*)
EMILY — Also drama major, lives in different dorm. Fascinated by Seymour; respects Nelson.
EPSTEIN — Their acting and playwriting instructor. Thinks Seymour is talented, but a pain-in-the-ass. Smart, ambitious, charming.

SETTING

Double room in college dorm. Two beds, lamps, dressers, desks, typewriters. Books about. Posters. Nelson's area neat, Seymour's a pig-sty. Two doors — one to corridor, one to john.

TIME

Early in 1981.

All programs and publicity materials for this play must carry the following notice:

COMMISSIONED AND FIRST PRODUCED BY ACTORS THEATRE OF LOUISVILLE

The Asshole Murder Case

AT RISE: House lights up. As scene is being set, actors wander in, chat with scene-changers. EPSTEIN Enters with folding chair, clipboard. He briefs actors, sets up chair.

EPSTEIN. Ready?. . . . places. (*He sits. Calls up to production booth:*) Okay . . . let's do the scene . . . *curtain!*

(*House lights dim. Stage lights up. NELSON at desk, goes over HELMER'S lines in "A Doll's House," acting version. SEYMOUR in john, door slightly ajar. After moment to establish, we hear:*)

SEYMOUR'S VOICE. (*from behind bathroom door*) Oh, Jesus!. . . . Oh, God!. . . . (*He groans.*). . . . where do they come from?. . . . I hope it's not from masturbation. . . . because I can't give that up! . . . (*He Enters room, wiping his face with towel; NELSON reading "A Doll's House"—does not acknowledge his presence.*) Hi, Nelson! (*NELSON reads.*) Reading . . . or faking it so you don't have to rrreally rrrelate to the ever-present roommate? (*NELSON reads on.*) D'you know what I was killing in there? (*removes towel from face*) Zits! See all these craters? (*puts his face up to NELSON's*) Zitsville! A fine upstanding community of zits—until I squeeezed 'em out! (*demonstrates*) Pow! Pow! Splaat! Ha ha . . . wait'll you see the mirror, Nelson. . . . them dead zits splattered all over it . . .
NELSON. (*not looking up*) Screw off!
SEYMOUR. Where is she?

(*SEYMOUR flings towel so it lands vaguely in his area. Goes over to phonograph, puts on Bob Seger's "No Man's Land"* and sings along with the first few bars or so. Then he flops down on his unmade, sloppy bed, without looking reaches under it, pulls out bag of Cheez Whiz bits, starts eating.*)

NELSON. Could you turn that cruddy music down?
SEYMOUR. Cruddy? (*no answer*) Did you say cruddy, Nelson?

---

*Cautionary Note: permission to produce this play does *not* include permission to use this song in production.

NELSON. You have total recall.

SEYMOUR. Cruddy??? Listen to this lyric. . . . (*Sings with record a bit.*) *"But sanctuary never comes/Without some kind of risk Illusions without freedom/Never quite add up to bliss"* (*record continues*)

SEYMOUR. (*speaks:*) That, Nelson, is *truth*!!!

NELSON. (*not without affection*) Your conception of truth is anything that comes out of a speaker and rhymes.

SEYMOUR. Nelson, I am trying to, you know, re-program your brain to the beliefs and customs of this society so you'll understand life!

NELSON. (*holds up Ibsen play*) There is more life in one sentence of Ibsen's than there is in that entire junky record.

SEYMOUR. Junk? You dare to call "No Man's Land" by the great and wonderful Wizard — Bob Seger — *junk*?

NELSON. *Dishonest* junk! Rock, hiding behind social concerns . . . to rip off people who goon-out over anyone who's shrewd enough to ring the right response bells — *BooHoo! I'm just a speck, lost in an un-caring cosmos! Ting-A-Ling!* Now, will you turn it off, please, so I can learn my lines before Emily comes to rehearse? (*returns to play*)

SEYMOUR. (*stops record*) There, asshole.

NELSON. (*not looking up*) Thanks, Seymour. You're a good shit and a munchkin.

SEYMOUR. (*after a beat*) Nelson, can I ask you a serious question?

NELSON. (*doesn't look up*) No.

SEYMOUR. Good. Here's the question: how can Ibsen, Luigi P., God — or *any* of them well-known playwrights — help you to understand life — you who are such a simple tool, you registered for the draft? (*No answer from Nelson.*) Hmmmm? There's a rumor goin' 'round the ol' campus that you, Nelson Perkins Winchester, the Third, registered for the draft!

NELSON. It's not a rumor.

SEYMOUR. Nelson, you've just made a reservation to fight their war.

NELSON. It's not war. It's not even the draft. It's simply registering your name. That is all. So in *case* of war . . .

SEYMOUR. You schmuck! Now your name's on their *list*!

NELSON. I take it you didn't register.

SEYMOUR. Hell no! I don't want them to know I exist.

NELSON. You better sign up. It's the law.

SEYMOUR. The law, Nelson, while originally created for common creeps like you and me, no longer exists for our benefit. Ah, no. The law is the mistress, pardon the metaphor, of the assholes who ride around in limousines with black-tinted windows. You know what I'm saying?

NELSON. You're saying you're totally paranoid.

SEYMOUR. . . . There's an old Buddhist dictum: "Skirt the authorities."

NELSON. It's impossible. They've got everybody on a computer someplace or other, driver's license, birth certificate . . .

SEYMOUR. I'll change my name. To . . . John Lennon. Nobody's using that name now.

NELSON. Seymour . . .

SEYMOUR. Name's John. (*Pantomimes playing guitar, sings a couple of lines of "Give Peace a Chance"*:*)

NELSON. . . . will you listen to reason?

SEYMOUR. (*Cockney accent*) I ain't a Yank, mate! I am a loyal subject of Prince Charles' mum, the Queen! God save the Queen's magisterial titties!

NELSON. Oh! You are really looking for trouble . . .

SEYMOUR. (*still Lennon accent*) I'm sick of living the myth!

NELSON. . . . you . . . *thrive* on making a rumpus, don't you!

SEYMOUR. (*still Lennon accent*) No bloody computer will control my destiny, asshole! Call me. . . . CAPTAIN INVISIBLE!!!! (*He makes himself invisible.*)

NELSON. They will find you!

SEYMOUR. (*still Lennon accent*) Not if I take all me frustrations and sufferings and go underground.

NELSON. That could be dangerous.

SEYMOUR. (*still cockney*) I'd rather die for something I believe in than for something I don't believe in.

NELSON. There's not gonna be a war, turdball.

SEYMOUR. (*out of hiding, real voice*) The economy's in the toilet, right? There's heavy unemployment, right? So, they need an excuse to tool up the factories. Plutonium! MX missiles! Nuclear subs! *BINGO*! Millions of jobs! Profits! I know what they're gonna do; my people keep me informed.

---

*Cautionary Note: permission to produce this play does *not* include permission to use this song in production.

NELSON. I take it you're still ballin' the anarchist with the big tits.

SEYMOUR. I saw a film *you* oughta see, then you'd understand the cyclic historic determinism. . . .

NELSON. I gotta read Mister Ibsen or Mister Epstein'll shoot me.

SEYMOUR. Epstein! He's one of *"Them"*!!! POW! POW! POW!

NELSON. Didn't he assign you a scene for tomorrow?

SEYMOUR. Yeah. . . . Hamlet. Plus he's making me *write* a scene.

NELSON. Then please do it, okay? and stop hassling me. I need a good grade this time.

SEYMOUR. (*still eating*) I'm thinkin' of cuttin' outa this hellhole for a while. . . . I mean why should my old man, who's economically terrorized, pay for me to lay around with the blahs an' munch out, y'know? Waitin' t'become a pawn in a real-life MONOPOLY game!

NELSON. I gotta study my lines, okay?

SEYMOUR. I dunno, maybe it's just that I'm on the rag today or somethin' . . . but I have come to the conclusion that you can't change anything in this society . . . political action is bullshit.

NELSON. Of course. So what do you do? Fight 'em with the weapon of art — *ergo* — your beloved truth!

SEYMOUR. (*Gets under covers.*) I can't relate to art. Or the theatre department. Make that the entire college. . . . a den of assholes.

NELSON. D'you think you might be categorizing?

SEYMOUR. Listen, you're working on "Doll's House." Can you identify with some old fart banker whose wife is a closet macaroon freak?

NELSON. (*laughs*) Don't get bogged down in details! Pay attention to the social situation which surrounds the play. The quintessence of Ibsenism is the shattering of illusions of the middle class. See, he wrote a lot about money . . .

SEYMOUR. If it's about money, you *know* it's the middle class . . . I mean, you ought to meet my father!

NELSON. (*back to play book*) Read Hamlet, willya? We'll bullshit tonight.

SEYMOUR. I can't relate to Hamlet; Hamlet owns Denmark.

NELSON. Seymour, you are the most self-oriented humanoid I have ever encountered on this mortal coil.

SEYMOUR. I don't wanta be controlled by the assholes who run this zoo!! They're tryin' to impose their ideas on me!

NELSON. *Perhumps* . . . they're merely trying to expose you to the great ideas of western . . . you know, open you up to. . . .

SEYMOUR. Last Tuesday! The scene I wrote for class? Epstein goes: "No, don't write that, write *this*!" That's totalitarian bullshit.

NELSON. Epstein didn't tell you what to write. Epstein said — "Quit hiding behind your theatricality and cleverness and try to do a simple, honest examination of a central problem."

SEYMOUR. (*his balloon somewhat deflated*) Hmmmn. . . . yeah . . . I guess he did say that, didn't he. . . . (*goes to his typewriter*)

NELSON. (*back to Ibsen*) You certainly are a hard-core turd. (*NELSON reads. SEYMOUR types a few moments.*)

SEYMOUR. GOT IT! The central problem, the thing which is poisoning our society — is *assholes*!

NELSON. (*He must now look up, of course.*) Assholes?

SEYMOUR. I'll do a scene about this disgruntled guy who gets up an Asshole Hit-List.

NELSON. (*matter-of-fact*) Seymour, you're crazy.

SEYMOUR. (*Intense, fingers poised over typewriter — as EMILY Enters.*) Who's the biggest asshole in America?

EMILY. Barry Manilow? (*She carries a copy of "Doll's House".*)

NELSON. *Emily*! Save me from this bizarre creep, who plans to walk into Epstein's section tomorrow and present him with — with — oh, God — YOU SELF-DESTRUCTIVE *IDIOT*!

EMILY. (*amused*) What. . . . what . . . ?

SEYMOUR. Epstein says deal with a problem in a direct way, so I'm gonna deal with a problem in a direct way.

EMILY. (*fascinated*) Tell Mama what you're gonna write fer ol' Eppie.

SEYMOUR. Scene 'bout a guy who makes a list of assholes then forms a hit-squad to assassinate them.

EMILY. Are you referring to the obvious assholes, or the underground assholes?

SEYMOUR. The hard-core assholes!

EMILY. Oh . . . (*a beat*) . . . OHH!!! I GOT A CANDI-DATE!!! *Tee-Bone Sigmeister*! OHHHH!!! He's a world-class!!

SEYMOUR. (*Types that name on list.*) Nominations are now open. Ah, how about . . . His Holiness, Doctor E. B. Winthrop Vail, President of this here asshole institution? (*Types in that name.*)

EMILY. (*still in her thought*) . . . ooooo. . . . *Sigmeister*! That diseased jock!

SEYMOUR. That's redundant.

EMILY. D'you know what he did? He got his stupid fraternity to hold this Christmas party . . . a *so-called* Christmas party . . . all female guests, right? And when we walked in . . . oh boy . . . we should have known it was gonna be a bad scene . . . but oh, no, all us sweet little innocents, you know, peace on earth and love thy neighbor . . . which is, you know, all that traditional crap our mothers brought us up on. . . . *OOOOHHHH*!!!

NELSON. Go on, we're all ears.

SEYMOUR. Speak for yourself, eunuch.

EMILY. . . . the Christmas tree was trimmed with condoms! Then those *assholes* dropped their pants . . . and we couldn't get out because they'd removed all the doorknobs!

SEYMOUR. *DEATH TO ASSHOLES*!

EMILY. *KILL*!

SEYMOUR. *We'll vacuum the dust-bin of the nation's soul*!

NELSON. You two are star-crossed.

SEYMOUR. The *New York Times* will be forced to report: *"ASSHOLE KILLERS STRIKE AGAIN!"* (*EMILY & NELSON laugh*)

SEYMOUR. (*continues Times story*) *"CLUES REVEAL VICTIMS HAD ONE THING IN COMMON — THEY WERE ALL ASSHOLES!"*

SEYMOUR. *"LEADING ASSHOLES FEAR FOR LIVES!"* (*NELSON shakes his head*) *"RICHARD NIXON DEMANDS PROTECTION"*

EMILY. (*sotto to NELSON:*) You know something? I don't think he's kidding!

NELSON. Can we return to Ibsen. . . . ?

EMILY. His madness knows no bounds: he sticks pins in meat-loafs and watches them die!

NELSON. Emily. . . . please?

EMILY. One look at his red, white and blue eyes and you know he's capable of anything!

SEYMOUR. These eyes are the envy of every doper on campus, (who reveres me as a pioneer on the frontiers of feral zonkitude!) (*EMILY cracks up with laughter. NELSON grabs her.*)

NELSON. For God's sake, we have got to rehearse this scene. . . .

EMILY. He sneaks into the chapel office at night and does it to himself on the Xerox machine!

NELSON. . . . . or Epstein is gonna crucify us!

EMILY. Ohhh. . . . all right. . . . (*She opens book.*)

NELSON AS HELMER. (*reads from play:*) "When did my squirrel come home?"

SEYMOUR. (*offers them Cheez Whiz*) You Norwegians want some munchies?

EMILY AS NORA. "Just now. Come out here, Torvald, and see what I've bought."

SEYMOUR AS NORA.. (*falsetto*) A whole stash box full of head goodies, Helmer!

NELSON AS HIMSELF. *TIME*!!!

SEYMOUR. (*goes to dresser drawer*) Anybody want a hit?

EMILY. Well, to tell you the truth. . . .

NELSON. No, please, we've got work to do. . . .

EMILY. If I work good, Torvald, can I have some after? Hmmmn? Can I?

SEYMOUR. (*like pusher*) Black beauties. . . . Oaxacan gold (a real skullfucker) quaaludes. . . .

EMILY. (*moves to see the stuff*) Oh, neat, I've never seen a quaalude. . . .

NELSON. Stay away from 'em — they're a dangerous downer!

SEYMOUR. Well, hey, don't you believe it . . . 'ludes are the vitamin C of fucking.

NELSON. Hey, maybe you better take your happy pills and blast off elsewhere. . . .

EMILY. Boys, boys, no fighting, no biting. . . .

NELSON. One of these days you're gonna push me to my limit, Seymour, you really are.

SEYMOUR. I know you guys ain't really workin' on Ibsen — you're workin' up to a little (*makes finger pantomime to indicate fornication*). . . .

EMILY. Seymour, shame on you! Ohhh! Such boorish macho arrogance. Right up there with Tee-Bone.

NELSON. (*mock weeping*) Why don't I assert myself and find a normal roommate?

SEYMOUR. Because you get-off on my incredible life-giving vibes . . . (*SEYMOUR hops about NELSON, vibrates fingertips, makes weird sounds.*) BLEEDY WEEDONK VRUBBLE ZONK VRIIIEEEEMMMM BEEPBEEP (etc.)

NELSON. (*Totally ignores him.*) Hi, Emily, what's new?

EMILY. Seymour? Oh *Seeeee*-more! Helloooo in there! (*SEYMOUR starts his life-giving dance and sounds about her.*)

NELSON. Watch, next he'll go into his famous gorilla number. (*SEYMOUR nips his fingers at her behind.*)

EMILY. Please don't. (*He continues.*) Cut, Seymour! (*He nips at her breasts.*) STOP IT! (*He continues; She swats him with her playbook.*) *Dammit! I don't like that!* (*He stops.*)

NELSON. Ignore the C-H-I-L-D.

EMILY. This boy has a real problem.

NELSON. Shall we get back to our I-B-S-E-N?

EMILY. (*still pissed*) I mean *real!*

NELSON. Okay, forget him. Ready?. . . . *Curtain!*

NELSON AS HELMER. "Is that my skylark twittering out there?"

EMILY. Oh boy, Seymour, you are rrrreally ill!

SEYMOUR. Face it, guys . . . ol' Henrik's "Doll's House" don't cut it no' mo'. People know about ladies walking out on their families. . . . my mother did it when I was 10! Playwright today's gotta shock his audience . . . gotta jazz 'em into reality. Le's do an improv. . . . show ya what I mean 'bout shocking the audience . . . (*to Emily:*) . . . . I'll be the Tampax, an' you be the vagina. . . .

(*EMILY and NELSON exchange looks simultaneously, toss play books away, move menacingly toward SEYMOUR. He, however, has become the Tampax and is not yet aware they approach.*)

SEYMOUR AS TAMPAX. Madam — d'you think someone in my shape might fit in here?

(*Then He sees them — gasps and pulls back in abject fear. . . . . all CHARACTERS freeze as lights slowly fade. Over this we hear BOB SEGER:*)

SEGER. (*sings: tape*) BUT SANCTUARY NEVER COMES/ WITHOUT SOME KIND OF RISK
ILLUSIONS WITHOUT FREEDOM/NEVER QUITE ADD UP TO BLISS
THE HAUNTING AND THE HAUNTED/PLAY A GAME NO ONE CAN WIN
THE SPIRITS COME AT MIDNIGHT/AND BY DAWN THEY'RE GONE AGAIN
AND SO IT SEEMS OUR DESTINY/TO SEARCH AND NEVER REST

TO RIDE THAT EVER CHANGING WAVE/THAT NEVER
  SEEMS TO CREST
TO SHIVER IN THE DARKEST NIGHT/AFRAID TO
MAKE A STAND
AND THEN GO BACK AND DO OUR TIME/OUT THERE
  IN NO MAN'S LAND

BLACKOUT

CHARACTERS un-freeze.
  EPSTEIN'S VOICE. *(from theatre) Okay. . . . lights, please!*

(ACTORS move D.C., *house lights up. EPSTEIN joins them,)*

EPSTEIN. Very nice, kids.
  SEYMOUR. *(now totally straight, nervous even)* Um . . . are
you talking about the acting, Mister Epstein . . . or, ha ha — the
writing?
  EPSTEIN. The acting . . . the performances were very
true . . . I believed everyone, though I'm not totally sure I like
the character you gave yourself, Seymour. . . . *(They ad lib
thank you's.)* I can't get into specifics just now, because I have to
leave for the Coast in about ten minutes . . . but I've got notes
for all of you that I'll give you in class Monday next. Meanwhile,
Seymour, I think you're finally starting to write directly to an
issue. . . . still a few too many irrelevancies, some bad
taste . . . and your usual gratuitous jokes. . . .
  SEYMOUR. The jokes make me feel secure. . . . also, I'm
scared of sounding, you know, corny. . . .
  EPSTEIN. Ha ha ha . . . you very cleverly Pirandelloed me,
I'm afraid. . . . the way you fitted my critiques into the
text. . . .
  SEYMOUR. Yeah, well, I didn't mean anything, you know, I
just thought it might be fun to try. . . .
  EPSTEIN. Is the sequence about not registering autobiographi-
cal to any extent? You don't have to answer that, of course . . .
  SEYMOUR. No, it's okay, yeah . . . that's more or less
true. . . .
  EPSTEIN. . . . . even though I'm an undercover agent for the
F.B.I.
  SEYMOUR. . . . . I'll probably go and register next week.
  EPSTEIN. Just pulling your leg, kid. Ah ha ha HA!
  SEYMOUR. Just pulling yours, sir! Ha ha ha ha . . .

100

EPSTEIN. Look, I have to catch a cab. . . . but before I go, Seymour, there's one thing I'm curious to know . . .

SEYMOUR. Yes sir?

EPSTEIN. Would your character have put *me* on his hit-list, d'you think?

SEYMOUR. Oh, no, sir!

EPSTEIN. Let's go for truth!

SEYMOUR. But sir, this is all make-believe! There's no hit list. Honest! (*to EMILY and NELSON*) Right, guys?

EMILY. Absolutely!   NELSON. Right!

EPSTEIN. Good. In that case, Seymour, your assignment for Monday is to re-write the scene—but leave out your damn hit list!

SEYMOUR. But sir, without the hit list, the scene will fall apart!

EPSTEIN. That's an interesting problem, Seymour.

SEYMOUR. I mean, that's what it's, y'know, *about*!

EPSTEIN. Work it out. (*He Exits*)

NELSON. Boy, you sure love to balance on the brink, don't you!

SEYMOUR. I don't work at it or anything. It just happens.

NELSON. You better watch it!

EMILY. I think you're charming, Seymour. The world needs heroes!

NELSON. If everybody just makes up their own rules, and flouts authority, where would that lead?

(*SEYMOUR is back in bed, hidden under the cover. He does not answer. NELSON goes resolutely to the bed, pulls cover off SEYMOUR's face.*)

NELSON. What would become of western civilization?

SEYMOUR. Pardon me, but you have obviously mistaken me for somebody who gives a shit.

(*He grabs a bag of Cheez Whiz, takes the bag under the blanket and covers himself from view. The lights gradually dim. His hand snakes out and turns on record player . . . music (no words) as lights go out on the last phrase of the instrumental.*)

THE END

Downtown

A One-Act

by

Jeffrey Hatcher

DOWNTOWN by Jeffrey Hatcher

1st Production December 14, 1987

Director. . . . . J. Christopher Wineman
Sets. . . . . Robert T. Odorisio
Lights. . . . . Lynn Lefkoff
Costumes. . . . . Susan Snowden

CAST

Brett. . . . . Malachi Bogdanov
J. . . . . Ale Weinberg
Saskia. . . . . Stephanie Phelan

PLACE

A corner booth at a downtown club.

TIME

Very now. Very late in the evening.

All programs and publicity materials for this play must carry the following notice:

COMMISSIONED AND FIRST PRODUCED BY ACTORS THEATRE OF LOUISVILLE

Downtown

As the house lights go down, the song plays through its first few bars, up to the end of the first reprise.

SCENE: Lights come up on a cavernous black space. Smoke and noise. Sound of people jostling and mixing. One piece of furnishing on stage: A large, comfortable circular booth and dining table. Black leather. Seductive. The table is crowded with bottles and glasses. Cigarette smoke hangs over the booth. The flash of neon lights and the occasional strobe pulse glares through the smoke, tinting the scene in sickly pastels every few moments.

AT RISE: Three people are seated at the table. BRETT, J., and SASKIA. All in their mid to late twenties. Very relaxed. Very poised. BRETT is tall and lean. His hair is high, silky, and moussed. Black shirt buttoned at the top. Sunglasses. Cigarette in hand. J. is small. Balding. A black t-shirt and over-padded black jacket. Sunglasses. Cigarette in hand. SASKIA is an icy blonde, her hair in a vicious cut. Chalky skin. Purple black lipstick. Jewelry. Black t-shirt. Sunglasses. Cigarette in hand. All three are drawling over the minefield of bottles, champagne flutes, and cocktails that crowd the table. Behind their black sunglasses, their eyes are focused on one corner of the club — somewhere Out Front. As the lights come upon this Dante-esque scene, crashing, dark, rhythmic dance music thunders through the club's sound system. It is, of course, not so loud that it drowns the dialogue.

BRETT. Look at her.
J. *Look* at her.
SASKIA. I thought she was *dead*.
BRETT. Have you read her reviews?
J. She's been dead for *years*.

---

*Cautionary Note: permission to produce this play does *not* include permission to use this song in production.

BRETT. Look at that *outfit*.

J. The *way* that she *walks*. . . .

BRETT. It's her all over. . . .

J. And coming out the side.

BRETT. *God,* she's embarrassing.

J. Embarrassing, *please!*

SASKIA. (*deadpan*) There are so many ways she can embarrass herself it must be difficult to choose just one.

J. The hips, the boots, the hair. . . .

BRETT. And that *outfit*.

SASKIA. She's like a tube of lipstick sweating gin.

BRETT. She's not a writer, she's an "event."

J. Perhaps her critics haven't seen her best work yet.

SASKIA. There's nothing she has the critics haven't seen.

J. Casting aspersion on her private parts?

SASKIA. My dear, she *has* no "private" parts.

J. She's derivative.

SASKIA. She is.

J. Not like your stuff.

SASKIA. Not like *yours*.

J. She *steals* is what she does.

BRETT. She had one good book a long time ago, when was it, last year?

J. The one about nuns.

SASKIA. Lesbian nuns.

J. A modern version of "The Song of Bernadette," only all the nuns were naked and without emotion.

SASKIA. Bold.

J. Right. Bold.

BRETT. Très, très, très bold.

J. I used to shop where she shopped. Had the same sack of groceries every Friday. Nothing but cigarettes, condoms, and anti-depressants.

SASKIA. It takes a lot to get through a weekend.

BRETT. She's dead.

SASKIA. She's dead.

J. Definitely. Dead. (*J. looks back and forth between Brett and Saskia.*) Is it time? Is it time?

SASKIA. (*Deadpan, not looking at him.*) No. It's not time. (*They shift in their seats and look in another direction.*)

BRETT. Check out the new boy.

SASKIA. He looks like a chauffeur.

BRETT. Look at his *out*fit! Is that a sharkskin suit?

J. I think it's a real shark's skin.

BRETT. *Look* at that *suit*. It's got a *reflection*! I can *see* myself in that suit.

J. You think it's too *much*?

SASKIA. Not if he had a gun and a partner with a gun.

J. What's his new book about?

BRETT. Probably another jaded, jaundiced, world-weary look at the glittering lifestyle, the pearl in the gutter, the cocaine and razor blades of the way-downtown scene.

SASKIA. A kind of modern "Madame Bovary" . . .

BRETT. A modern "La Bohême". . . .

SASKIA. A modern "Faust". . . .

J. Only the characters are all naked and without emotion.

BRETT. It's book club sales are doing *great* in Westchester.

J. Why not, he's derivative.

BRETT. Derivative.

J. Derivative is what he is.

BRETT. Not like *your* stuff.

J. No, not like *yours,* either.

BRETT. He's dead.

SASKIA. He's dead.

J. Definitely. Dead. (*They shift again to look in another direction.*)

J. Uh-oh.

BRETT. Uh-oh.

J. Enter the "wunderkind."

BRETT. Oh, *my.*

J. What a *face*!

BRETT. What a *dresser*!

J. What a *charmer*!

SASKIA. What a *guy*.

BRETT. (*Beat. A lower voice.*) He's *such* a fraud.

J. He's *so* dis*gust*ing.

BRETT. So re*volt*ing.

J. He's the *worst*.

BRETT. The *absolute.*

J. The nadir of nadirs.

BRETT. A dis*as*ter without penultimate.

J. The stingiest . . .

BRETT. . . . the gaudiest. . . .

SASKIA. He's looking this way. (*They all look up and blow "him" a kiss.*)

ALL IN UNISON. Kiss-kiss! (*They huddle in low voices again.*)

J. Did you read his latest?

BRETT. I didn't read it, I *lived* it.

J. Was it awful!

BRETT. It was like a week at the Men's Room at Grand Central.

SASKIA. Only naked . . . and without emotion.

J. I haven't seen him in the clubs recently.

BRETT. I haven't seen him in the clubs lately.

J. Some places won't let him in anymore.

BRETT. Some places bar the door.

SASKIA. I saw him at the opening of "Innertube."

J. Really?

BRETT. What's "Innertube" like?

J. It opened last Thursday.

SASKIA. It's already dead.

BRETT. It's dead.

J. Everything's dead.

BRETT. Did you go to "The Drainpipe's" opening last night?

SASKIA. No, it's dead.

BRETT. (*nods*) It's dead.

J. Definitely. Dead.

BRETT. (*looks out again*) He's here with his agent.

SASKIA. Yes, he's here with "The Dwarf."

J. Look at the Dwarf.

BRETT. He's like an endomorph.

J. He's like an exposed muscle.

SASKIA. He's like a hernia in a suit.

BRETT. He's gone downhill.

J. How can you tell?

BRETT. He used to represent movie stars.

J. He used to represent the best.

SASKIA. He used to represent Cheever and Updike, now he represents the decline of the West.

J. I wouldn't let him represent *my* stuff.

BRETT. I wouldn't let him represent *your* stuff either.

J. Nor yours.

SASKIA. Nor yours.

J. He's . . . he's. . . .

BRETT. Derivative.

J. Derivative.

SASKIA. For an agent, he is.

J. Dead.

BRETT. Dead.

SASKIA. Definitely. Dead.

J. (*look to both of them*) Is it time? Is it *time*?

SASKIA. (*Deadpan, not looking at him.*) No. It's not time. (*They look in a different direction.*)

BRETT. Look who's here now.

J. It's the *Vanity Fair* girls.

J. The *nerve*.

BRETT. The *gall*!

SASKIA. (*sing-song*) Bitch-bitch-bitch, bitch-bitch-bitch. . . .

J. (*waspy*) Oh, are there *six* of them?

BRETT. They came with Pajama.

J. Pajama?

BRETT. Pajama Dombrówicz.

SASKIA. Just wrote her bio. She's twenty-two. Called *Native New Yorker*.

BRETT. And like a lot of native New Yorkers, she's from Nebraska.

J. I think she's copied your stuff.

SASKIA. You *do*?

J. I think she's stolen your thunder.

SASKIA. You *do*?

J. I think she's plagiarized your best stuff from here to "down under."

BRETT. But it's not *like* your stuff.

J. No, not *like* yours at all.

BRETT. She steals.

J. Yes, she steals.

BRETT. Yes, she steals from us all.

J. (*Looks at BRETT*) Not like your stuff.

BRETT. (*To J.*) Not like *your* stuff.

J. (*after a beat, to BRETT*) Well, actually, a *little* like your stuff.

BRETT. (*blinks*) Pardon?

J. Well, I mean . . . it's *kind* of like your stuff.

BRETT. That's what I said, she steals from us all.

J. Well. . . .

BRETT. Well, what?

J. Well. . . .

BRETT. *Well, what*?

J. You have the same views. You have the same concerns.

BRETT. Yes.

J. A similarity in style.

BRETT. Yes.

J. Subject matter.

BRETT. Yes.

J. Jokes. . . .

BRETT. Yes.

J. . . . number of pages per book. . . .

BRETT. Yes.

J. . . . preference for jacket covers. . . .

BRETT. Yes, *so*!

J. Well . . . *she was* there *first*.

BRETT. (*a beat*) Getting there *first* doesn't prove she didn't steal it from *me*.

J. But if she didn't steal it from you . . . *until* she started writing the same things that *you* wrote . . . then what did she steal if she wrote it first *before*?

BRETT. (*biting off the words*) She steals in retrospect. Are you suggesting *I* stole from *her*?

J. No!

BRETT. Are you suggesting I lifted styles?

J. No!

BRETT. Dialogue?

J. No.

BRETT. Characters?

J. No.

BRETT. Plots?

J. No. . . .

BRETT. Well! All right then!

J. (*thinks a beat*) There *was* her first book. . . .

BRETT. Yes . . .

J. Your first book. . . .

BRETT. Yes . . .

J. It's a little like *her* first book.

BRETT. There are *no* similarities between *her* first book and *my* first book!

J. Of course not. (*beat*) Her first book got published.

BRETT. *My* first book was published!

J. No, it wasn't.

BRETT. Yes, it was!

J. It wasn't *sold*.

BRETT. *(sputtering)* It was *bound*!

J. It was *stapled*.

BRETT. Anything *else* I've stolen from her?

J. Uh, no, no, not *you*. *(to SASKIA:) You,* maybe, *(to BRETT:)* but not you.

SASKIA. I beg your pardon?

J. Well. . . .

SASKIA. What did I steal?

J. Well. . . .

SASKIA. *Well what?*

J. Well, there was your second book.

SASKIA. My second book. . . .

J. Your second book *was* . . . her *third* book.

SASKIA. My second book was her third book? Proves my point!

J. Except her *third* book came before your *second* book.

SASKIA. Her book was completely different!

J. From . . . ?

SASKIA. From what?

J. Which book? All your books are alike.

SASKIA. *(fuming)* My second book was different from her third book!

J. Which came before your second.

SASKIA. *My* book was about a group of gay Khymer Rouge refugees who emigrate to South Africa to open a For Profit Penal Colony run by lepers and dwarfs. *Her* book was about a group of gay Khymer Rouge refugees who emigrate to South Africa to open a For Profit Penal Colony run by lepers and *midgets*! There *is* a *difference*!

J. I'm just saying there was similar subject matter.

BRETT. And style.

J. And dialogue.

BRETT. And opening lines . . .

J. And ending . . .

SASKIA. My book was a *meditation* on an earlier work!

BRETT. What earlier work?

J. *(points at Pajama)* Her third book.

SASKIA. It was a "re-thinking!"

BRETT. *(deadpan)* It was a re-typing.

J. We're not saying you stole.

BRETT. We're not saying you borrowed. *(beat)* We're not saying.

SASKIA. What are you implying?

BRETT. Why, what are you inferring?

SASKIA. If I infer what you're implying, then we know what the implications are.

BRETT. How do you know what we imply if you haven't already inferred what we imply?

J. Because she infers *first*.

SASKIA. I've never attacked *you*!

BRETT. I haven't attacked *you* either.

SASKIA. (*to J.*) And I haven't attacked you *either*!

J. No. No. No, you've *copied* me a little, but you haven't *attacked* me. Recently.

SASKIA. When did I attack you!

J. Well . . .

SASKIA. When did I attack you!

J. In print?

SASKIA. Yes, in print!

J. In print, never, no. No, never in print. They wouldn't print what you called an attack.

SASKIA. As if you've never criticized me!

J. Where?

SASKIA. In print!

J. In print?

BRETT. I wouldn't say he's never criticized you.

J. No.

SASKIA. No.

J. No.

SASKIA. When did you criticize me in print?

J. Well. . . .

SASKIA. What did you publish?

J. It wasn't published.

SASKIA. It wasn't published!

J. I . . . *withheld* it from publication.

BRETT. That means he couldn't sell it.

SASKIA. The only way you could sell criticism of me would be if you put it on the back of an umbrella and sold it in a rainstorm.

J. Plagiarist!

SASKIA. I don't plagiarize!

J. Neither do I!

BRETT. Neither do I!

SASKIA. I never steal anyone's dialogue!

BRETT. I never steal anyone's dialogue either!

SASKIA. Of course not!

BRETT. Of course not!

J. I have integrity!

BRETT. I have integrity!

J. As a journalist!

BRETT. As a journalist!

J. I have integrity! Yes!

BRETT. Yes! (*beat*) As a "journalist?"

J. What . . . ?

BRETT. A "journalist?"

SASKIA. Get a shovel. . . .

J. I consider myself a journalist in the mode of Henry Adams, George Orwell, and Truman Capote!

SASKIA. That's only because Adams, Orwell, and Capote can't *sue.*

J. Who wrote the first articles on the Lower East Side?

SASKIA. Who wrote the first articles on "attitude."

BRETT. And Post-Modernism!

SASKIA. And the club scene!

BRETT. And the galleries!

J. And the "downtown" world! (*Stand-Off. They are all nose-to-nose. Beat.*) Well . . . well, it wasn't any of *us*, but who wrote them *next*! (*They all look a bit shamefaced and uncomfortable.*) Uh, is it time?

BRETT. (*looks off*) Shut up.

J. (*to SASKIA:*) Is it time?

SASKIA. (*moping*) Shut up.

J. (*After a pause.*) I didn't mean to insult you.

SASKIA. (*unconvinced*) Sure.

J. (*to BRETT:*) I didn't mean to insult *you.*

BRETT. (*grumbling*) Sure.

J. (*Looks back and forth for a moment.*) Is this gonna be the start of one of those famous literary feuds, like Mailer and Vidal?

SASKIA. Could be.

BRETT. It's a good guess.

SASKIA. Which do you want to be, Mailer or Vidal?

J. Because . . . we're probably more useful to one another if we stay together. In a union. In tandem. In concert. Solidarity.

BRETT. Solidarity?

J. We're a group. A school of thought. A style. Like the Bloomsbury Group or Provincetown or The Cedar Tavern. We can't break up over a little difference about "who stole-*influenced* who." Can we?

BRETT. Sure we can.

SASKIA. Yeah, I think so.

J. We're part of a generational wave. Writers of a time and place, of social complexity and cultural communality. If we dissolve, so much goes with us. Huh? Agreed?

BRETT. All right. Agreed. So?

J. Well . . . so . . . forgiven?

SASKIA. Forgiven? Well . . . well . . . all right. Forgiven.

J. Forgiven?

BRETT. Yeah, yeah, I forgive us, too.

J. And we're all friends again?

BRETT. Solidarity.

SASKIA. Solidarity. (*They all clink glasses.*)

J. As artists, as writers, as leaders within our craft and community.

SASKIA. (*more chipper*) Yes!

BRETT. Yes!

J. Yes! (*Drinks. Beat.*) Is it time?

BRETT. (*glances at watch*) Yes. I think it's time now.

J. (*beginning to rise*) As writers . . .

SASKIA. (*rising*) . . . artists . . . .

BRETT. (*Sliding out of the booth.*) . . . and leaders.

J. (*standing now*) Yes.

(*We see now that BRETT and J. are wearing aprons at their waists. They take up two trays. SASKIA picks up two large menus from the table, turns Down Front and, with a pearly smile, says:*)

SASKIA. Good evening. Table for two?

BLACKOUT

THE END

Electric Roses

by
David Howard

ELECTRIC ROSES by David Howard

1st Production May 17, 1988

Director. . . . . Andrea Urice
Sets. . . . . .Paul Owen
Lights. . . . . Lynn Lefkoff
Costumes. . . . . .Kevin McLeod

CAST

Russ. . . . . .DEL PENTECOST
Sara. ADRIANNE KRSTANSKY
Darrell. . . . . .WAYNE E. PYLE

SETTING

A bus station and a cell in a county jail.

All programs and publicity materials for this play must carry the
following notice:

FIRST PRODUCED AT ACTORS
THEATRE OF LOUISVILLE

Electric Roses

(SCENE: *The scene reflects two different locations. The first is the waiting area of a bus station in Yuma, Arizona. Seated on a bench in this area is SARA. She has a suitcase sitting on the floor next to her. She wears slightly heavy make-up, which covers a few bruises on her face. The second area is a cell in a county jail, although it may be suggested by only a straight backed chair. On the chair sits RUSS, SARA's husband. The two never see one another. They exist together for the audience's convenience.*)

RUSS. (*For the most part, his tone throughout the play is fairly reflective. He addresses the audience directly.*) The day I married Sara it was so hot, you could'a fried an egg on the hood of my truck . . . musta been a hundred and five — hundred and six, maybe . . . Course, there's nothing special about that . . . it was June . . . It's funny how things can stick in your mind, isn't it? Three years ago, an' I can still almost feel it. . . . Shit it was hot . . . So me an Darrell was drinkin' beer . . . Guess there's nothing special bout that either. . . .

(*DARRELL, RUSS's best friend, appears in the other area. SARA sees him. There is a tense silence between them.*)

SARA. . . . Hello, Darrell.
DARRELL. (*quietly*) Hi.
SARA. . . . What are you doing here?
DARRELL. Lookin' for you.
SARA. Why'd you come here?
DARRELL. Looked everywhere else . . . saw your truck.
SARA. It's not mine, it belongs to Russ . . .
DARRELL. Well . . . yeah.
RUSS. I guess I drink too much. I know that . . . I'd be lying if I didn't say it scared me sometimes. (*He thinks a moment.*) So, where was I? . . . Oh, yeah, it was hot, an' Darrell says, "Why don't we go to Vegas?" An' I said, "When?" An' he said, "Right now!" (*SARA sits back down.*)
DARRELL. I saw Russ, too.
SARA. When?

DARRELL. This morning.

SARA. Yeah?

DARRELL. Yeah. (*pause*)

SARA. How is he?

DARRELL. You haven't seen him?

SARA. No.

DARRELL. Umm . . .

SARA. (*quietly*) . . . didn't think it was such a good idea.

DARRELL. . . . yeah . . . he feels pretty bad.

SARA. (*thoughtfully, sincerely*) I know he does.

DARRELL. He'll be out by noon.

SARA. I'll be outta here by then.

RUSS. You ever been to Las Vegas? . . . It's something, I'll tell you. . . . You gotta go at night, though. All those lights, shit, it's something. (*He laughs a little.*) Somebody said they musta built it at night, cause it's so damn ugly in the day. An' Darrell said the only thing you ought to do in Las Vegas is eat. You try to do anything else, they're just taking your money . . . Course, you can drink for nothing if you gamble, but . . . I suppose he's right anyhow . . . you can't drink enough to make it worthwhile. (*SARA takes out a cigarette.*)

SARA. You gotta match?

DARRELL. (*as he takes out some matches*) Shouldn't do that, you know. It can kill you. (*She laughs, as he lights her cigarette. As she laughs, she grimaces a little and holds her side.*)

SARA. Ohh . . .

DARRELL. You all right?

SARA. Yeah . . . just breathed in too much. (*She stops a moment, closes her eyes and holds her side.*)

RUSS. So, we figured, you know, what the hell, you gotta do something, you can't just sit there . . . an' you know as well as I do there's nothing to do here in Yuma at night . . . Shit, the sun goes down, this place turns into a damn grave yard. Feel like you're in Tubac or somewhere.

SARA. You know, Darrell, if you hadn't been with him last night, I could be dead now. (*DARRELL stands uncomfortably, not answering.*) You talk to Abby last night when you got home?

DARRELL. No, she was asleep.

RUSS. So, he called Abby, an' we went to get Sara. She was working. She works over at Jerry's Tastee Cone . . . Used to be the Tastee Freeze, til they run outta money. Now it's the Tastee Cone . . . An' we go over there, an' said, you know, we're goin' to Vegas. You wanna come?

SARA. Took me three minutes to get down the stairs this morning.

DARRELL. . . . You look good.

SARA. Yeah?

DARRELL. Yeah, you can hardly tell.

SARA. (*She smiles slightly.*) Thanks . . . I don't like to wear so much make-up.

DARRELL. I know . . . but, it looks okay . . . kinda sexy.

SARA. (*as she laughs*) Darrell, you always were full of shit.

RUSS. An' she said, "I gotta change my clothes. I can't go to Las Vegas with hot fudge all over me. So, we went to Darrell's and got Abby and then went over to pick up Sara . . . an' . . . (*He thinks a moment.*) When she came outta her place, she'd . . . fixed herself all up . . . see, she was good at that, real good . . . I can still see her in my head. (*He pauses again.*) I guess I will for the rest of my life.

DARRELL. So . . . where you headed? (*SARA shakes her head.*) Come on, Sara.

SARA. Darrell, if he figured you knew, he'd get it out of you one way or another.

DARRELL. . . . yeah, I suppose he would . . . north?

SARA. I guess.

DARRELL. . . . don't go to your sister's. That's the first place he'll go.

SARA. I'm not stupid, Darrell.

DARRELL. Yeah . . . sorry.

RUSS. You see, a woman like Sara . . . I mean, she was pretty an' all, but . . . that ain't it. It was like, when I looked at her, something happened . . . (*He puzzles over what he feels.*) She put a hook inside of me that wasn't ever gonna let go . . . I knew that . . . I knew that the minute it happened.

DARRELL. You need money or something?

SARA. No.

DARRELL. I can run over to the bank. Only take a minute.

SARA. No, I'm alright.

DARRELL. You sure?

SARA. I'm fine. (*pause*)

DARRELL. Well here. (*Takes $10 out of his wallet and hands it to her.*) Let me buy you lunch . . . . wherever . . .

SARA. (*resignedly*) Thanks, Darrell. (*She takes the money.*)

RUSS. You know, I woke up this morning, an' my hand was busted . . . it was all wrapped up, an' it hurt like hell. (*He examines it a moment.*) An' I looked at it, and I thought, "What the hell's happened to you?" You know? Did that ever happen to you? You know, where you wake up, and there's something different, and you didn't even know it?

DARRELL. What are you gonna do?

SARA. I don't know. Get a job, I guess.

DARRELL. Well . . . you can always get a job in Vegas. It's easy to work there, I hear.

SARA. (*looks at DARRELL*) . . . I'll keep it in mind.

DARRELL. You know, Sara . . . (*not sure about continuing —he does anyway*) . . . you're the best thing that ever happened to Russ. (*pause*) This is gonna kill him. You know that, don't you?

SARA. I can't think about that. (*pause*)

DARRELL. I just want to know if you're sure, that's all.

SARA. If I wasn't sure, I wouldn't be here.

DARRELL. (*quietly*) Yeah.

RUSS. So, anyway, we're drivin' up there. We're out there in the desert, up past Needles, an' you know, there ain't nothing out there. It's just black. An' Darrell pulls the car over, and, I don't know, runs off to take a piss or something, an' me and Sara get out of the car. . . . Abby was asleep. She always does that in the car . . . An' you know, there's nothing around. . . The only light you've got is from the stars. And I'm telling you, you look up and you look up and you can see things you never believed were up there . . .

SARA. (*troubled*) It's not just this, you know . . . not just . . . last night.

DARRELL. I know.

SARA. (*begins to cry a little*) Sometimes, it would scare me to go out of the house, the way he'd look . . . I felt I couldn't breathe, you know?

DARRELL. Sara, you don't have to tell me nothing. (*A pause. SARA looks at a diamond necklace which she wears around her neck.*)

SARA. You remember when he bought this? (*DARRELL nods.*) In Vegas?

DARRELL. Yeah.

SARA. I remember, he took me outside to show it to me. And he held it in his hand up over my head. And I could see it glittering there in the dark . . . you couldn't see nothing but the light sparkling on it. And he said, "You know what that is, Sara?" And

I said, "What?" An' he said, "That's you. That's what you are to me."

RUSS. We were standing there, an' I could feel her there next to me . . . that dark all around us. And I said, "You know why we're going to Vegas, don't you?" And she said, "Why's that?" And, I said, "So I can marry you." An' she said, "Bullshit." An' I said, "I am. I'm takin' you to Vegas, and I'm gonna marry you when we get there." And she laughs, and she says, "Why in the hell should I marry you?" And I said . . . (*His tone becomes much more significant — the words mean considerably more.*) I said, "Cause no one in the world is ever gonna feel what I feel for you right now." (*There is a pause.*)

DARRELL. (*frustrated*) God damn it! . . . You know things would be a lot easier if you could just tell him to go to hell, you know?

SARA. Yeah . . .

DARRELL. Just tell him to go screw himself.

SARA. Yeah . . . (*pause*)

DARRELL. Not that easy though, is it?

RUSS. Hell, I don't know what was in her head to say yes to me, but she did. I guess maybe she knew how much I wanted it . . . (*He thinks a moment.*) First thing we did when we hit town was find a place that would do it for us. You know, they've got places that will do it all night. An' we found one . . . this little white house with electric roses that lit up the outside, an' . . . I married her.

DARRELL. You know what Abby's gonna do to me when she finds out I was here, don't you? Hell, it might be better if I got on the bus with you. (*In spite of herself, SARA smiles. Mock seriousness.*) You know, you're ruining our social life, don't you? I mean, shit, who's Abby gonna play cards with?

SARA. She can call Cheryl Ann.

DARRELL. The hell she will. Cheryl Ann's not coming in my house. She's nothing but trash, cheap trash. (*SARA laughs.*)

DARRELL. Well, she is.

RUSS. Later on, we were sitting in this bar . . . Darrell's eating shrimp cocktail. You know, forty-nine cents. An' Abby's over playing the nickel slots. An' this guy . . . this ass-hole, keno player . . . He's got this shirt with flowers all over it, and his hair looks like . . . you know, Mr. California-Dude. An' he's sittin' there lookin' at Sara . . . just staring at her, an' you know what

I'm talkin' about . . . Shit, I wanted to break his greasy neck. An' I said, "What are you lookin' at, pal?" An' he says, "Do you own her?" An' I said, "Yeah, I do." And then I broke his fuckin' nose. (*Over a speaker, we hear the voice of the bus station announcer.*)

ANNOUNCER. Ladies and Gentlemen, the Trailways bus for Blythe, Lake Havasu, Las Vegas and all points north is now boarding outside the terminal. Would all passengers ticketed for this route please make your way to the boarding area.

RUSS. If you could'a seen what he was doing . . . what his eyes were doing. . . . (*He stops to think.*) What he wanted . . . shit if he were here now, I'd break it again, looking at her like that. (*SARA stands, grabs her suitcase and begins moving out to the bus.*)

SARA. (*as they look at one another*) Well, I guess I better . . .

DARRELL. Yeah . . .

RUSS. See, you gotta understand, a woman like that, geez, if you could see how they are around her. (*As SARA moves to the exit.*)

DARRELL. (*His voice stops her Exit.*) Sara . . . ?

SARA. Huh?

RUSS. I start thinking about that, and . . . something happens inside of me.

DARRELL. (*He speaks with a pain in his voice.*) Umm . . . (*He thinks a moment.*) I guess I'm just gonna miss you, that's all. (*She looks at him for a moment, then crosses to him and embraces him. They are both near tears.*)

RUSS. (*It is painful for him to speak.*) I admit it . . . I've hit her . . . (*Pause. He looks over the audience.*) Well, what do you want me to say? I'm not proud of it . . . Sometimes, when I drink . . . all them looks . . . (*quietly*) Sometimes, you just wonder how strong a person is, you know? (*As DARRELL and SARA part.*)

SARA. You take care, Darrell.

DARRELL. Yeah.

SARA. Tell Abby goodbye for me.

DARRELL. I will. (*SARA crosses to the exit. She turns before she Exits.*)

SARA. (*As she cries*) I love him, you know that.

DARRELL. Yeah, I know.

(*The lights begin to fade on the bus station, it becomes nearly a sillouette as RUSS finishes.*)

RUSS. God knows, I love her . . . She's the most important thing in the world to me . . . she knows that, too. No matter what happens, she knows it.

THE END

4 a.m. (Open All Night)

by

Bob Krakower

4 A.M. (*Open All Night*) by Bob Krakower

1st Production May 17, 1988

Director. . . . . Bob Krakower
Sets. . . . . .Paul Owen
Lights. . . . . Lynn Lefkoff
Costumes. . . . . .Kevin McLeod

CAST

MAN. . . . . .ALE WEINBERG
JIM. . . . . .CHRIS BURMESTER
DOC. . . . . ROB CAMPBELL
WOMAN. . . . . PAMELA STEWART

CHARACTERS

MAN—A nice guy, a semi-regular at this diner.
JIM—The guy behind the counter, he knows Man and Woman.
   Very empathetic and insightful.
WOMAN—A nice gal, a semi-regular at this diner.
DOC—A regular. He is a little smashed, but never violent. A dry
wit, a big heart.

SETTING

An all-night diner.

TIME

4 A.M. an April evening.

NOTE

The play moves at a brisk pace. Pauses only where noted.

For Kathleen

All programs and publicity materials for this play must carry the
following notice:

FIRST PRODUCED AT ACTORS
THEATRE OF LOUISVILLE

124

4 A.M. (Open All Night)

SCENE: One table, two chairs. A simplified counter, 3 stools.

MAN. I'm not hungry.

JIM. Coffee?

MAN. Ah, shit —

JIM. (*pours coffee*) What's the matter?

MAN. I'm outta smokes —

JIM. How many times I have to tell you, buy the carton — not the box.

MAN. I know, but, and see, that's another thing — she hates that I smoke —

JIM. So —

MAN. Like lickin' an ashtray, she says, but I don't wanna quit —

JIM. So don't quit —

MAN. I'm gonna quit.

JIM. (*offers cigarette*) Here ya go.

MAN. Thanks.

JIM. (*lights cigarette*) So —

MAN. So anyway that's my point.

JIM. What is?

MAN. That we don't communicate —

JIM. No, you communicate —

MAN. No, we don't.

JIM. Oh, yes, you do pal. You communicate. You don't *agree,* but you communicate —

MAN. Hey, if she doesn't *understand* me, than how can you call that communication?

JIM. Look, do you understand the words I'm speaking?

MAN. Jim, your missin' the point —

JIM. No, I'm not. (More coffee?)

MAN. (Yeah)

JIM. Do you understand what I am *saying*?

MAN. Look, we're just wrong for each other, that's all —

JIM. Do you?

MAN. Yeah —

JIM. Make sense to you?

MAN. Yeah —

JIM. Do you agree with me?

MAN. No —

125

JIM. So we *disagree*—

MAN. Yeah—

JIM. But you *understand.*

MAN. So?

JIM. So that's what I'm sayin—You say—"I get up, I come down here for a burger, have a little bit of Joe, bum a smoke—no harm done."

MAN. That's right.

JIM. She wants you safe at home.

MAN. That's right—

JIM. She disagrees.

MAN. That's *wrong.* She doesn't *understand.* This is what I'm trying to tell you—Every fuckin' time. I get up, I can't sleep, right? I'm restless—wanna have a smoke, I don't know, just walk around or something, get centered or—no, I don't mean "get centered," I mean, well—you know?—I don't know— Anyway, the house feels stuffy, my head's a fuckin' windtunnel and I wanna be *outside,* ya know, in the air, I don't know—clear my mind, or something. Goddamn it, I can't pinpoint it, I just felt out of sync, I felt trapped—like, I don't know, I just don't belong there next to her and,—

JIM. You wanna be with her or not?

MAN. Yeah, yeah, I *do*—I guess, she's great, it's just that I *got up,* ya know and I start tippytoeing out of the room—'Where you goin?" she says. "Diner," I say ('cause that's where I'm going)— "For what?" she says—"I don't know, get a burger," I say— "No", she says. "No, what?" I say "No," she says—"No, I can't go?" I say—"Nooooo" (and I hate the fuckin' way she says that, like she's got some kind of insight into the true meaning of my soul that *I* have yet to discover.) "Nooooo," she says "you're lyin'—you ain't *just* 'goin'-to-get-a-burger'." "I'm not?" I say, "Funny, that's what I *thought* I was doin'." (*Enter WOMAN, with newspaper.*)

WOMAN. Hey, Jim.

JIM. Be with you in a second, kiddo.

WOMAN. You got change for cigs?

JIM. Yeah—(*Pause as JIM pours her a cup of coffee. MAN & WOMAN notice each other.*)

WOMAN. Thanks.

MAN. Where was I?

JIM. You were leavin' the house.

MAN. Oh yeah, right, so—"Listen," she says, "We got chopmeat here. Stay, I'll *make* you a burger" — "But I wanna go *out*," I say — (*WOMAN Exits, leaving coffee on table*) "Stay and *talk* to me," she says, "What's on your mind" — "Honey. I'm going to the diner." "Liar." — *Liar?* I mean I'm here, aren't I? So then, I feel *bad*, see, 'cause I just wanted some air, but I don't want her to be *mad*, so I decide to *stay* — she then tells me I'm stayin' for the wrong reasons and yells at me to *go*. And the next thing I know *I'm* fightin' to stay in the apartment and she throws me out! I mean, help me out here — Can't a guy get into his car, roll down the window, turn up the radio, drive down to the local burger-hole (sorry, Jim), pop a quarter in the box, sing "Under the Boardwalk" (perhaps the greatest song ever recorded) and pound down on a burger without being accused of I-don't-know-what?

JIM. So you *do* communicate.

MAN. You *don't* understand.

JIM. Oh I understand — She just wants you to *talk* to her. Have you ever had an affair?

MAN. What, cheated on her?

JIM. No, I mean ever, in your life?

MAN. Yeah.

JIM. Has she?

MAN. I think so.

JIM. So —

MAN. So what?

JIM. So she's working off a perception she has of this event based on life experience —

MAN. What event?

JIM. A man disappearing in the wee hours of the morning for seemingly no particular reason, you idiot. It's perfectly natural.

MAN. But I'm not *doin'* anything —

JIM. *I* know that.

MAN. Why doesn't she know it?

JIM. You tell me. (*WOMAN re-enters wearing walkman, singing to herself.*)

MAN. So what am I supposed to do?

JIM. I don't know — Find someone who likes to eat burgers and drink coffee at 4 o'clock in the morning.

MAN. Oh yeah — Great — Like who?

JIM. Like her — (*WOMAN lights a cigarette.*)

MAN. Oh, come on —

JIM. She smokes —

MAN. (*looks at her*) No, it wouldn't work.

JIM. How do you know that?

MAN. I can tell. Anyway—I'm not in the market.

JIM. You're happy where you are—

MAN. Yeah—

JIM. So what are you doin' down here at 4 o'clock in the morning? (*pause*)

MAN. She's taller than I am.

JIM. Everybody is.

MAN. Fuck you, Jim.

JIM. You haven't even met her—

MAN. (*looks at her again*) I got somebody—

JIM. I know, who doesn't understand you. Listen, Mr. Nice Guy, if you got somebody, go home—you got a bed, lie in it. If not—

MAN. If not, what?

JIM. Let me ask you something—you happy?

DOC. Unbefuckinlievable.

JIM. (*overlapping*) So what are you doin' down here at 4 o'clock in the morning?

MAN. I just want a fuckin' hamburger and a cup o' joe, okay?

JIM. I don't see you eatin' anything. (*pause*)

MAN. What am I gonna say to her, I got nothin' to say. We got nothin' in common—

JIM. Well, for starters, you're both here at 4 o'clock in the morning for the same reasons—

MAN. You don't know that.

JIM. Bet ya a fin—

MAN. Forget it.

JIM. Then go home.

MAN. I don't want to go home.

JIM. Why not?

MAN. I just want a fuckin' hamburger!!!

DOC. You got chopmeat at home.

MAN. This is ridiculous.

JIM. Why did you come down here?

MAN. To be alone.

JIM. Take a look around you—

MAN. Yeah?

JIM. You alone?

MAN. Jim, let me tell you something—if you're really perceptive, you can tell within about 10 seconds of meeting someone if the chemistry's there—

JIM. Yeah, I can tell it ain't there, I can tell by the way you can't help staring at her since she walked in the door.

MAN. Hey, I have *some* experience with this kind of thing . . . give me some credit.

JIM. Your full o'more bull, pal, than the chopmeat in your fridge. (*MAN turns to stare at WOMAN.*)

DOC. Problems with your girl?

MAN. No.

DOC. Liar.

MAN. What is going on tonight?

DOC. You're lying, ain't you — you have problems with your girl.

MAN. Yeah, so?

DOC. I'd say that makes you a liar.

MAN. Who is this? Who the fuck are you?

DOC. I'm trying to communicate something to you here, pal —

MAN. I left my apartment and walked straight into the Twilight Zone — I just want a fuckin' hamburger!!! Jesus Christ, what is this, a goddamn conspiracy — what is going on here tonight? I just want a fuckin' hamburger!!!!! (*Gets up and goes to the men's room. WOMAN removes headphones.*)

WOMAN. Hey Jim, a burger and another cup of coffee, please —

JIM. A very popular item tonight.

WOMAN. What do you mean?

JIM. Nothin'. Anything else?

WOMAN. No, just a glass of water.

JIM. Sure.

WOMAN. And some more cream. . . .

JIM. Okay . . .

WOMAN. . . . um, Jim? (*JIM turns.*)

WOMAN. Who's the guy?

JIM. Which guy?

WOMAN. The guy — he was just sitting over there.

DOC. I think he went to relieve his conscience.

JIM. He had a fight with his future ex-girlfriend.

WOMAN. Oh.

JIM. Why?

WOMAN. I think I've seen him around, ya know — here and there, ya know?

JIM. Yeah?

WOMAN. Oh, I don't know, skip it. I don't know . . . I don't know. You got a light?—Thanks. I got this feeling like I've met him before, like I *know* him, but I haven't, so—

JIM. So?

WOMAN. I can't explain it.

DOC. Explain what?

WOMAN. I don't know . . . Déja vu? Some *connection,* I don't know, skip it. Where's the paper?

DOC. Sometimes I think we're all just facing in the wrong direction and if we just turned around and faced each other we'd all find exactly what we're looking for. —I mean, why is it I can sit here and look you dead in the eye and know exactly what you should do, but when I look at myself, I don't have a fuckin' clue?—nothing. Why is that?—Why is it that I'm smarter about your life than I am about my own—you ever think about that? I do—why is that—who am I talking to?? (*pause—they stare at him*)

JIM. So you think he's cute?

WOMAN. I didn't say that—

JIM. I ain't asking for a commitment—Come on, I'll introduce you—

WOMAN. No, that's okay.

JIM. Then why did you ask?

WOMAN. I don't know why—

JIM. Come on—I'll introduce you . . . Why not?

WOMAN. We wouldn't get along—

JIM. You haven't even met him.

WOMAN. Let me tell you something, okay? Intimate sexual relationships—

DOC. Excuse me?

WOMAN. —of course, it depends on the quality—distort your perceptions of time and space. You become irrational, single-minded, thick-brained and stupid, and tend to smile out of context occasionally. Articulation becomes a struggle. I can't get any work done—I'm absent-mindedly stroking my thighs in public and bruises appear on my body, and I wonder, "where did those come from?" I eat less, smoke more, and drink by the bottle, not the glass. I become witty as hell—I mean, you feel so BLONDE. Man, *Cosmo* magazine becomes appealing and those little love quizzes take over as the single source of outside information—and then before you know it you start to feel pretty damn good about yourself—

JIM. Sounds terrible.

WOMAN. —and then you look up one day to find—he's gone. So, no.

JIM. No what?

WOMAN. I don't want to meet him—

JIM. So why did you come down here?

WOMAN. To be alone.

JIM. Take a look around you— (*pause*)

WOMAN. Let me ask you, what would I have in common with a guy like that?

JIM. A guy like what? You don't even know him—

WOMAN. He's shorter than I am.

JIM. Why do you do this to yourself?

WOMAN. Okay, just for argument's sake, let's say, I say hello—

JIM. Yeah—

WOMAN. He comes over—

JIM. Right—

WOMAN. We talk—

JIM. Hmm hmm.

WOMAN. Our eyes connect, he becomes vulnerable—

JIM. Now you're cookin'—

WOMAN. He puts his life in my hands, I start to care for him—

JIM. Go, baby, go—

WOMAN. He opens up and lets me in, my life starts to revolve around him—I *love* him with everything I have—

JIM. Well—

WOMAN. —and wake up one morning to find he doesn't *know* me.

JIM. Well, whose fault is that?

WOMAN. "I don't know, I don't have any idea who you are," he says, and he's right, of course, because I've spent all my time holdin' *him* up and he gets scared and pulls away—and then he's gone and there I am—

JIM. Whoa—

WOMAN. —right back down here at this damn little table—

DOC. Hey, kiddo.

WOMAN. —and I feel like I'm takin' my life in my hands just by sayin hello, ya know? I mean I've been around the block a few times, I think I can save myself this one trip.

JIM. What if this *one* trip was the *right* trip? (*pause*)

WOMAN. Jim, let me tell you something — if you're really perceptive, you can tell within about 10 seconds of meeting someone if the chemistry's there.

DOC. Unbefuckinlievable — if this was a movie, nobody'd believe it.

WOMAN. Look, I came down here for a burger and a cup of coffee. If I want a dating service, I'll go somewhere else.

DOC. It's amazing anybody meets anybody.

WOMAN. Please, I'm sorry, this whole thing, I don't know why I mentioned it —

JIM. I think I do.

DOC. Why is everybody so tense!?! Just say hello —

JIM. What are you afraid of?

DOC. It's not gonna kill ya!

WOMAN. Well, let's start with rejection and go from there.

DOC. You afraid he might *like* you? That it? (*pause*)

WOMAN. Okay, okay, okay — I'll tell you what — I'll make you a deal —

DOC. Okay —

WOMAN. I'll make you a deal — I'll count backwards from 100 and if he turns around and says hello to me before I get to one, then I'll know it was meant to be, okay?

JIM. Okay.

DOC. Okay.

WOMAN. Okay. (*breath*) Now, may I please have a cup of coffee and the newspaper?

JIM. (*smiling*) One joe on the move —

DOC. Madam, your paper. I'll just keep the sports.

(*WOMAN puts headphones on and tries to read the newspaper as she counts backwards. MAN re-enters.*)

MAN. So what's the answer?

DOC. What's the question?

MAN. What we were talking about *before* —

DOC. Two Hearts Are Better Than One.

MAN. What say?

DOC. Two Hearts Are Better Than One, at Belmont in the Eighth.

MAN. What are you talking about?

DOC. (*Nodding toward the woman.*) I got a gut feeling.

MAN. What are the odds?

DOC. 100 – 1.

MAN. A little high, wouldn't you say?

DOC. I got a gut feeling.

MAN. How does she run in the mud?

DOC. What's the difference?

MAN. You've got to take everything into consideration—
You've got to figure—

DOC. Figure what?

MAN. Rain, odds, jockey—

DOC. No, too much trouble.

MAN. What do you mean?

DOC. Too much thinking.

MAN. You gotta *think* about it.

DOC. No, you think, you start to doubt . . . too much room
for error.

MAN. And if you fail?

DOC. I fail. What are you, Mr. Perfect?

MAN. No—

DOC. You need to be right all the time?

MAN. You need all the information to help you figure it out.

DOC. All that shit does is keep you from laying down a bet.

MAN. But you gotta base your bet on something.

DOC. I do.

MAN. On what?

DOC. My gut.

MAN. And what does your gut say?

DOC. *Always follow* your *instincts*.

MAN. You wager money, just based on a hunch?

DOC. No, not a hunch, *an instinct, a feeling.*

MAN. You bet on your gut?

DOC. No, I bet on a horse, and I'm betting the bank on Two
Hearts Are Better Than One.

MAN. (*to JIM:*) Come on, help me out here—

DOC. Hey, I'm trying to tell you something here, pal, and you
ain't listening, You don't listen, is your problem.

MAN. I listen.

DOC. No, you don't, you *think*, but you don't listen.

MAN. Listen, I like thinking, okay? . . . You have to think
through what you listen to.

DOC. I don't have to think of anything.

MAN. But what if you're wrong?

DOC. If I'm wrong, I'm wrong . . . *I'm* not afraid to be
wrong—I *learn* from my experience, I'm still betting, my instincts get better, I'm *making* money, *losing* money, but I'm

doing something. Every day I'm doing something, what are *you* doing? If I did it your way I'd never win, never lose, probably never lay a bet. I'd just be buried in the newspaper all day. You bet horses?

MAN. No.

DOC. Didn't think so. Ever think about?

MAN. Yeah—

WOMAN. 47 . . . 46 . . . 45, (*etc.*)

JIM. I'll bet you a sawbuck you can't.

MAN. What? (*JIM points to girl.*) I can't.

JIM. Why not?

MAN. I'm not that kind of guy—

JIM. What kind?

MAN. The kind that, ya know, I'm not—I can't—I mean, I haven't. Listen, I don't want to bother anybody, ya know, EVER, so, ya know, just too much heat in the kitchen.

JIM. Listen, friend, honestly, you're feeling the heat before you're seeing the light.

MAN. Say again?

JIM. If Michael Jordan was always looking at the guys in his way, he wouldn't be able to see the basket, understand?

WOMAN. 29, 28, 27, 26, . . .

MAN. I'm not equipped for this—

JIM. You know, you've given me lots of reasons why you shouldn't do this, except one.

MAN. What's that?

JIM. A good one.

MAN. What difference does it make to you?

JIM. I get tired o'lookin' at lonely faces that don't need to be that way, come on—

DOC. Take a chance.

JIM. It's just hello.

MAN. Sayin hello is like taking your life in your hands, ya know? It fuckin' scares me to death . . .

DOC. Every time.

WOMAN. 18, 17, 16, . . .

JIM. If it were me, you'd want me to ask her out—

MAN. Yeah. But what if I—

DOC. For Chrissakes come on already!!!!

MAN. Okay, okay, okay, I'lla, I'll tell ya what I'll do—

JIM. Come on come on!

MAN. That's it, I'll count to ten, see—

DOC. Let's go let's go!!

MAN. —and turn, I'll turn and if she's lookin' at me, I'll take my shot.

Doc. Count fast!

MAN. Okay, okay, okay (*closes his eyes, breathes*)

MAN.   1   WOMAN.

                                 2   6

                                 3   5

                                 4   4

                                 5   3

                                                                      2

                                                        (*The other men
                                                        stand and lean
                                                        in.*)

                                                                      1

                                 6
                    (*She stands, looks at him.*)

                                 7

                                 8
                    (*She crosses to the door.*)

                                 9
                    (*She looks back at him.*)

                                 10
                    (*He starts to turn, hesitates, takes a
                    breath.*)

                    (*She leaves.*)

                    (*He turns, she's gone.*)

Doc. Way to go, smart guy.

(*MAN slowly moves toward the door, looks out the window and slowly waves goodbye as "Under the Boardwalk"* begins to play softly. Lights fade.*)

THE END

*Cautionary Note: permission to produce this play does *not* include permission to use this song in production.

Americansaint

A Play

by
Adam LeFevre

AMERICANSAINT by Adam LeFevre

1st Production May 26, 1987

Director. . . . . Bob Krakower
Sets. . . . . .Paul Owen
Lights. . . . . Cliff Berek
Costumes. . . . . .Kevin McLeod

CAST

Brother Vincent. . . . . .DAVID GARCIA
Bettina Smooches. . . . . .JENNY ROBERTSON
Captain Mike*. . . . . NICK PHELPS
Arlo Pennypacker*. . . . . KEVIN FABIAN

SETTING

Various, at sea and in Vermont.

TIME

1903.

All programs and publicity material for this play must carry the following notice:

FIRST PRODUCED BY ACTORS
THEATRE OF LOUISVILLE

----

*may be played by the same actor.

Americansaint

SCENE 1: Burial at Sea.

CAPTAIN MIKE. Et cetera, et cetera, and so we commit his soul to the deep. (*He lifts the board and a body slips from under a shroud and falls down into the sea.*) Ung-ah!

BROTHER VINCENT. Wait!

CAPTAIN MIKE. Kerplunk. What is it, Padre? Did you want to say a few words? Oops. Looks like I jumped the gun. Oh, my backbone! He was a big one.

BROTHER VINCENT. Now he's light. God will lift him.

CAPTAIN MIKE. Worse case of *mal de mer* I ever seen. Well, go ahead and say your piece. Don't mind there's no body. It's the thought that counts. I got to get back to the poop, though. The mate can't chart a course for beans. Got us turned toward Terra Horribilis.

BROTHER VINCENT. Bless you, Captain.

CAPTAIN MIKE. And vicey versa to you, Padre. Elmo! Steady as she goes, I says! You got bilgewater for brains, boy!

BROTHER VINCENT. (*kneels*) Dear Lord, grant me the strength to finish alone the work you set before Father Dominick and myself, his humble novice, whom no one could blame if I just turned around and went right back to the Vatican because my stated duties were strictly secretarial and the unlettered world abashes me, but now, should I pluck this flower it is solely to *my* credit, and then, who knows what elevation? so I will forge on to find this child of God and confirm her saintly deeds so that we might greater glorify your name here on earth, and, who knows? though I desire no honor other than to better serve you, I would certainly be somebody in Rome. Arrivederci, Padre. In Jesus' name we pray. Amen.

CAPTAIN MIKE. (*off*) Land ho!

SCENE 2: On the Road

BROTHER VINCENT, exhausted and dusty, plops down his duffle near a signpost of three arrows. One says "Brattleboro." One says "Rutland." One says "Peru."

Brother Vincent. Lord! The roads of America are long.

(*BETTINA SMOOCHES, a girl of 13, comes skipping down the lane, stopping periodically to scratch the dust with her stick. She sings a little ditty.*)

Bettina.
I love
Eddie Stalinky.
I wear
his face on my pinky.

Brother Vincent. Hello, little girl. What are you doing with that stick?

Bettina. Looking for something I want. (*She sings.*) I love Eddie Stalinky . . .
Can you touch your tongue and your butt? I can. (*She touches her tongue with the finger of one hand, and her behind with the finger of her other.*) Ha! This is Vermont, you know.

Brother Vincent. How far to town?

Bettina. Over the bridge and round the bend. Hey! "Railroad crossing. Look out for the cars. How do you spell it without any *R's*?" *I-T.* Ha! Get it? My brother taught me that one. He's home in bed, dying from diarrhea. I found a snake with two heads. Wanna see?

Brother Vincent. That's terrible.

Bettina. It's dead, don't worry.

Brother Vincent. I mean your poor brother.

Bettina. He'll be dead too, before sunset. So will you— someday. Me too. I can see the future sometimes. Plain as my hand.

Brother Vincent. What is your name, child?

Bettina. Bettina. Bettina Smooches. But someday it will be Stalinky. I just know it.

Brother Vincent. Are you the one they call the Virgin of the Valley?

Bettina. Are you kiddin'? I'd smack 'em. If you give me a nickel, I'll show you my bellybutton. There's some-body's face in there. Guess who? Oops, I got to go. My brother just died. Here's my stick. It's magic, so don't point it nowhere lest you mean it. Just a loaner, you understand, case you need some magic. 'Bye, now.

SCENE 3: The Telegraph Office

(VINCENT Enters with duffle and stick. He rings bell for service.)

BROTHER VINCENT. Hello? Anybody there? Hello? Somebody?

ARLO. Right you are. I was readin' out back. *Plutarch's Lives.* Gonna be President someday, or bust tryin'.

BROTHER VINCENT. I'd like to send a telegraph.

ARLO. I'll show these pumpkin heads a thing or two. Be statue of me right next to Ethan Allen in the square. All right, stranger, let 'er rip.

BROTHER VINCENT. Arrived in America and Peru . . .

ARLO. Peru, Vermont. A nice place to live if you got no ambition. Me, I got bigger fish to fry. Go ahead.

BROTHER VINCENT. May have located the Virgin of the Valley. Stop.

ARLO. Stop?

BROTHER VINCENT. There's more.

ARLO. Let's hope so.

BROTHER VINCENT. How must phenomena be confirmed? Please advise. Stop. Sad . . .

ARLO. Wait. Lucky for you I got a little Greek. All right, go on.

BROTHER VINCENT. Sad to inform Father Dominick died at sea. Sign it Brother Vincent, and send it off to the Vatican.

ARLO. Rome?

BROTHER VINCENT. Correct.

ARLO. I ain't punched nothin' through the cable since McKinley got shot. Jeezum Crow, what a treat!

BETTINA. *(Enters)* Mister? I need my stick.

ARLO. Get out of here, Goo-goo Eyes! You already been told.

BETTINA. I need my stick. Daddy wants me to fetch Silas back. Says he didn't finish his chores. How I feel about it don't matter. Daddy is Daddy, simple as that.

BROTHER VINCENT. Here, child.

BETTINA. Holy smokes, be careful! I figured a man wearin' a dress ought to know which is the business end of a stick. Guess I pulled a boner. Well, no harm done.

ARLO. Has I got to call the constable, Goo-goo Eyes?

BETTINA. Name's not Goo-goo Eyes, you crook. Oops. A duck just ate a June bug gonna make him choke. Bye, now. *(Exits)*

BROTHER VINCENT. Is she the one they call the Virgin of the Valley?

ARLO. She's been called just about everything. Kinda famous around here.

BROTHER VINCENT. Is it true that in her presence statues have wept tears of blood, and the crippled have jumped up and danced?

ARLO. Well, she's a caution, I'll tell you that.

BROTHER VINCENT. Did not a local haunt of Sodomites, an avowed parlor of harlotry, recently, spontaneously burst into flames when the girl walked by?

ARLO. That'd be Ethel Mae Houligan's. They couldn't for sure pin that on Goo-goo Eyes, but, tell you this—I wouldn't leave that child and her curiosity alone in the same county with a box of matches.

BROTHER VINCENT. Where does she live?

ARLO. Down the road, same as everybody.

SCENE 4: In The Air

BETTINA. You can't see me. You don't even know I'm here, and that's just the way I like it. Shh. (*She makes radio noise—squeaks, hums, static.*) Come in. Come on in out of the in-between. Shh. It's a long ways off, but, if you listen, you can hear time begin. It sounds like . . . Shh. Come in now. Come on in. (*She makes radio noise.*)

SCENE 5: Goin' Fishin'

(*LEM SMOOCHES Enters with a fishing pole.*)

BROTHER VINCENT. Mr. Smooches?

LEM. Maybe. Fishin' helps me think.

BROTHER VINCENT. I'm Brother Vincent, agent of the Holy See in Rome.

LEM. "And Jesus said unto him, 'I will make you a fisher of men.'" Well, he weren't talkin' to me. I'm a fisher of fishes. A nuts and bolts believer, honest enough to call a misery a misery. Born up on that there mountain. Or that one. Hard to tell. Cloudy.

BROTHER VINCENT. Bettina is your daughter?

LEM. Some years ago my wife took off with an auctioneer, so I'm somethin' of a doubtin' Thomas.

BROTHER VINCENT. She's a remarkable girl.

LEM. You know Doris?

BROTHER VINCENT. Doris?

LEM. Doris. What? She changed her name?

BROTHER VINCENT. I'm referring to Bettina.

LEM. Oh, Goo-goo Eyes. She's remarkable, all right. Been that way ever since her brother near drowned her in the duck pond.

BROTHER VINCENT. I've been sent by the church to confirm the wonderments of which we have heard.

LEM. Come again?

BROTHER VINCENT. Is it true she has caused the crippled to jump up and dance?

LEM. Well, her own brother she did once, when she laid that stick into him. See, Silas was kicked in the . . . how can I put it? . . . gonadals by a milkcow when he was three year old. Upshot of it was his left arm and leg quit growin'. He got on okay cause as the rest of him growed, we tied a milkin' stool to his bum side to even him out. He's down to the duck pond one day, chuckin' rocks at the frogs and turtles like a boy'll do, and Bettina, she got Christian names for all them critters, so she took her stick to 'im. He danced all right. That's when he decided to drown her.

BROTHER VINCENT. There are reports of statues she touches weeping blood.

LEM. Well, I wouldn't doubt it.

BROTHER VINCENT. Did you yourself ever see such a wonder?

LEM. A statue, you say? Not actually. I did see her make a tomcat *piss* blood, though. Her and that stick.

BROTHER VINCENT. Is it true her mere gaze caused a brothel to burn?

LEM. If you're speakin' of Ethel Mae's, that's the first I heard that particular theory. If'n it's true I'll take a strap to that girl. Every man needs his horns scraped somehow, and, whatever else Ethel Mae may have been, and that, I repeat, is her own damn business, she was always a clean woman, rest her soul. Smelled like strawberries she did.

BETTINA. (*Enter with stick*) Hard as I smack him, Silas jest won't get up.

LEM. Course not. The boy is dead. He's crossed over. He's gone.

BETTINA. Where's he gone to, then?

LEM. A better place than this, bet your face on it. Where his limbs is all one size and he don't need no milkin' stool to stand straight.

BETTINA. Hey, Mister. Wanna try? (*She extends the stick to him.*)

LEM. Put that stick down, girl, and tell me true. Did you set Ethel Mae's on fire?

BETTINA. I never done nothin' but walk on by.

LEM. Did you gaze at it?

BETTINA. I did. One time. Yes, I did.

LEM. And what did you see?

BETTINA. Flames. Flames of many colors, like the tongues of angels. And they was prettier than the privy lilies and Black-eyed Susans.

BROTHER VINCENT. Praise God. They'll make me a bishop.

LEM. If I thought it'd make one lick o' difference I'd whup you senseless. 'Scuse me, Roman, I'm off to wet a line. Leave the boy alone, girl. He's dead. (*Exits*)

BROTHER VINCENT. How blessed I am to have found you. Dear child, do you know? God is in you.

BETTINA. Whereabouts? (*She looks for him.*)

BROTHER VINCENT. You have great and wonderful power.

BETTINA. Truth is my stick ain't workin' like it should. Silas won't budge.

BROTHER VINCENT. You shall be known around the world as Saint Bettina, Virgin of the Valley.

BETTINA. No sir, I shall not. I shall be known as Mrs. Eddie Stalinky. We will be married between the wars in a cathedral made entirely of music. And I will wear his name proudly as my own skin right to the stone on top of my grave. The rest is all turtle talk. Hey! Can you touch your tongue and your butt? (*He does.*) You're learnin', mister.

SCENE 6: Back in the Telegraph Office

(*BROTHER VINCENT sits eating an apple. ARLO Enters, loaded with books.*)

ARLO. This country needs a man in the White House who knows his hydraulics as well as his history. Not to mention poetry. Been readin' poetry to sharpin' my tenderness. *Poetry is the alibi of the soul.* I thought that up myself, and you may quote me.

BROTHER VINCENT. It's odd, but, you know, I've begun to feel at home here. I'm beginning to understand how peace passeth all understanding. Perhaps, when I'm a cardinal, I'll return to supervise the building of a shrine. That little girl is going to be a saint, you know. The rest is just formalities.

ARLO. Too bad you never met Ethel Mae. Now there was a saint. Trust ya till payday. Oh, by the by, somethin' come in for you last night on Elroy's shift. Asked me to get it to you. (*ARLO hands him a telegraph message.*) What's the matter? Is the spellin' off? Elroy is a chowderhead at spellin'. Here. Bet I can translate for ya. (*takes message and reads*) "You are lost. Stop. Virgin of Valley proved hoax by parish priest two months ago in Peru, South America. Stop. You are lost. Stop. Find your way home." Signed, Cardinal Quisadicci. Peru, *South* America. Oops. Looks like you pulled a boner. The 3 : 15 out of Brattleboro will get you to Boston by morning. Here, read some hydraulics along the way. Put some color back in them cheeks. I'll look you up on my European tour.

SCENE 7: On the Road and in the Air

(*BROTHER VINCENT trudges by with duffle.*)

BETTINA. Hey, Mister. I know where you're goin'. I kin see the future sometimes, clear as this day. Ever since Silas drowned me in the duck pond. He pushed my face right down there in the turtles and the lilytails, and held me there till a bubble burst in my head. You're goin' home. And you'll live there a long time — longer than you want. And, on a snowy morn there in the Eternal City, you'll die in your bed wonderin' if the things I said is true. They're true. You ain't never gonna be Pope, nor cardinal, nor titmouse, but that's all right. Cause it was meant that way. They will be wars and wars and wars, and children will have children, and children will have beasts, and beasts will take numbers for names. And somewhere between the wars, on a day not unlike this one, I will marry Eddie Stalinky, clown prince of radio. And our children will make music at the wedding out of tubes and bones. And they will decide in the middle of the music not to be born, for the sake of his career, for they will understand, as only the unborn can, how important it is. And then at the darkest hour of midnight, when the whole world thinks the sky is comin' down, he will make the people laugh. And the laugh will be deep and round, and for a moment the world will be like one person. And when he dies folks will say, "All of us have died a bit today." It was meant. I was born to be his bride. Ladies and gentlemen, Mr. Eddie Stalinky, Clown Prince of Radio. This is what he told me on our wedding day. "Someday, my little airwave, you will understand everything. Clear as the hand on your face."

(She puts her hand on his face and that is the end of the play.)

THE END

Watermelon Boats

A short play

by

Wendy MacLaughlin

WATERMELON BOATS by Wendy MacLaughlin

1st Production May 8, 1979

Directors. . . . . Larry Deckel and Michael Hankins
Sets & Lights. . . . . Marcia O'Grady
Costumes. . . . . Anne E. Winsor

CAST

KATE. . . . . CYNTHIA JUDGE
KITTY. . . . . MARY JOHANTGEN

CHARACTERS

KATE.
Tan, thin, and healthy. She wears jeans, button down shirt and
sweater tied around waist.
KITTY.
Rounder, softer, and more feminine. She wears peasant blouse,
full skirt and two braids tied with ribbons.
They age from eleven to twenty-one in the course of the play and
change hair styles as indicated in the action. The action takes
place on the shore of a lake at three different moments over a ten
year span.

All programs and publicity material for this play must carry the
following notice:

COMMISSIONED AND FIRST PRODUCED BY ACTORS
THEATRE OF LOUISVILLE

WATERMELON BOATS

AT RISE: KATE and KITTY sit on step ladders facing the lake which is located where the audience sits. Both hold watermelon boats, hollowed-out melon rinds with candle masts. All props are imaginary and use of them is mimed.

KITTY. (*face front*) How much longer?

KATE. (*checks watch*) Twelve seconds. Oh, help, your candle went out. (*Mimes lighting a match on jeans.*)

KITTY. (*cupping candle*) Thank heavens you brought more matches.

KATE. Five, four, three, two, one. . . . push them off. (*They each push a boat into the water and watch them sail.*)

KITTY. (*blows a kiss*) Bon Voyage.

KATE. (*waves*) Good luck.

KITTY. How many do you think there are?

KATE. A million at least. But ours is the best.

KITTY. All the others look like stupid watermelons.

KATE. Aren't they gorgeous?

KITTY. Fabulous.

KATE. Fantastic.

KITTY. The best watermelon boats we've ever made.

KATE. With the candles they look like stars dancing across the water.

KITTY. Sir Galahad sailing out to sea in search of The Holy Grail.

KATE. Mine'll be first across I bet.

KITTY. Why?

KATE. It's smaller. The wind'll pick it up.

KITTY. They look the same to me.

KATE. The secret's in the cutting.

KITTY. (*preening*) Kate, notice something?

KATE. No.

KITTY. I'm wearing a bra.

KATE. I'm never going to wear one.

KITTY. My mother says you'll look like a cow if you don't.

KATE. I like cows.

KITTY. Hanging to your knees.

KATE. She just says that to scare you so when you have breasts you'll smash them all down.

KITTY. Ummmm. (*unbraiding hair*) Who do you think we'll have for sixth grade?

KATE. Mr. Hawkins, I hope.

KITTY. Me too. He has neat eyes. Every time he looks at me I have to go to the bathroom. Did you know I was born nine months after my brother died?

KATE. Exactly?

KITTY. He died January ninth. I was born October ninth.

KATE. (*incredulously*) They did it the day he died?

KITTY. I can't believe boys put that. . . .

KATE. The whole idea is gross.

KITTY. I wonder what it feels like.

KATE. No boy is ever going to do it to me.

KITTY. Never?

KATE. Well maybe if I get married, but I probably won't because of my career.

KITTY. There're still pictures of him all over the house. My father wanted me to be a boy.

KATE. Mine, too.

KITTY. Doesn't that just make you furious? (*frustrated with her hair*) Why does Mother braid my hair so tight?

KATE. Here, let me help. (*unbraids Kitty's hair and mimes brushing*)

KITTY. Thanks. You've been my best friend since first grade. Isn't it amazing we've been coming to this lake for six years? Am I yours?

KATE. My what?

KITTY. Best friend.

KATE. Sure.

KITTY. Do you have a lot of best friends?

KATE. Some.

KITTY. Don't you think it's weird we're best friends and we're both named Katherine?

KATE. Lucky everyone calls you Kitty and me Kate.

KITTY. Kitty's a funny name.

KATE. Perfect for you.

KITTY. I like Kate better.

KATE. When I'm a great writer everyone'll call me Katherine.

KITTY. Like Katherine Mansfield.

KATE. Who?

KITTY. "I want by understanding myself to understand others." She wrote that in 1922. In her journal.

KATE. Oh . . . yes.

KITTY. I have total recall. People with high I.Q.'s usually do.

KATE. (*impressed*) You know your I.Q.?

KITTY. Ah-huh.

KATE. How?

KITTY. Once I looked it up in Miss Porter's office.

KATE. What's mine?

KITTY. That's not my business.

KATE. But you know it.

KITTY. I might.

KATE. Then tell me.

KITTY. I shouldn't.

KATE. I'll tell Miss Porter if you don't.

KITTY. Weeeeeelllllll . . . I don't remember exactly but it's lower than mine.

(*Fog horn blows. KATE stops brushing and fixes her hair.*)

KITTY. If this fog ruins the race I'll die. I can't even see our boats. Oh there they are. Look, Kate. (*no answer*) Kate? You're still mad.

KATE. (*cold*) I'm not but the rest of the class is furious. We had a chance to win the Drama High School Cup three years in a row.

KITTY. It's just a stupid play. I'm sorry, Kate. I know you wrote it and it's very good but . . . .

KATE. It would have looked good on my college transcript.

KITTY. I'm sorry. I told you to give me sets. I'm good at art. Why'd you make me be that brainless maid?

KATE. Come off it, Kitty. You died to be the maid. The maid got to wear the cute costume.

KITTY. Well no one told me she had any lines.

KATE. Only one.

KITTY. You know I freeze in front of people.

KATE. Four words. Four simple words and you screw them up.

KITTY. My parents must have gone through the floor with embarrassment. God, I wish I had a drink.

KATE. I've told you a million times, every ounce of liquor you drink destroys ten thousand brain cells.

KITTY. Who cares about my brain anyway? Boys certainly don't.

KATE. You really make me mad, you know it? When are you going to grow up? Really, Kitty. When?

KITTY. (*imitating*) Really, Kitty. When? You sound exactly like my parents. Grow up, Kitty, be like Kate. Kate has her feet on the ground. Kate has a head on her shoulders. I don't want to be like you. I want to be me. Anyway I can't be you, can I? Boy, am I insecure. Guess it's because I haven't had my period in two months. (*a laugh*) You don't think I'm pregnant do you?

KATE. Two months isn't very long.

KITTY. I stopped the pill.

KATE. Damn.

KITTY. Who wants to get cancer?

KATE. Who wants to have a baby?

KITTY. I can always get an abortion.

KATE. Don't be crazy.

KITTY. I don't have the vaguest idea who the father might be. Can't imagine any of the imbeciles we know being a father. Can you?

KATE. You've got to stop sleeping around.

KITTY. I can't. I mean, I don't want to.

KATE. Have some respect for yourself.

KITTY. I like it.

KATE. You like being used? That's what they're doing, you know. You might just as well be a urinal.

KITTY. It's not like that. When I'm close to a boy . . . really close, I feel important. For a time someone needs me. I'm connected to someone, part of the same thing. Afterwards, though, at home in bed. . . . I feel more alone. (*pause*) Kate, do you think there might be a real person growing inside of me? A little body with fingers and toes?

KATE. Why do I feel responsible for you?

KITTY. Promise you'll come with me if I have to have an abortion.

KATE. I'd do anything in the world for you but that.

KITTY. You have to.

KATE. I can't. It's wrong.

KITTY. I would for you.

KATE. Abortion is wrong.

KITTY. What'll I do?

KATE. I'm sorry, Kitty. I have to follow my conscience.

KITTY. You're really hard, Kate. You know it?

KATE. If having principles is hard. . . .

KITTY. Even here . . . in the spring, at the lake. I'm all relaxed but you're still so tight. Thin . . .brown . . .

KATE. I wish I could help you.

KITTY. Thin . . . brown and hard. Year round.

KATE. So be it.

KITTY. Very dull.

KATE. What?

KITTY. Thin. . . . brown and hard. Year round. It's very dull. Boooooorrrrrrrrring.

KATE. (*tight lipped*) Sorry.

KITTY. Maybe in your senior year you should let go a little. Maybe. . . . smile at a guy.

KATE. Too disciplined, I guess.

KITTY. Well brought up.

KATE. Probably.

KITTY. Or afraid.

KATE. Afraid?

KITTY. You might spoil the image. Perfect woman. Nobly planned.

KATE. Well, it's late. I have to go.

KITTY. I bet you spend the night thinking of lines you won't cross. Perfect stays on one side looking down her nose at the rest of us screwing it up on the other.

KATE. (*turns to go*) Goodnight, Kitty.

KITTY. (*grabs her arm*) And you think you're going to be a writer? That's a laugh. Who's going to read you? You don't know the first thing about life.

(*Foghorn blows. They change hair styles.*)

KITTY. (*shivers*) Ohhh it's getting cold. (*They put on sweaters.*) Not even a moon. But look, the first star is out. Sometimes I think there're people just like us up there thinking we're a star. Oh God, Kate, promise you won't write that in your first book. Everyone'll think I'm psycho.

KATE. I doubt I'll write one page, much less a book.

KITTY. You're kidding.

KATE. No.

KITTY. You're going to be a famous writer.

KATE. Who says?

KITTY. You've always said.

KATE. Changed my mind.

KITTY. You can't do that.

KATE. Stop staring at me.

KITTY. I counted on you.

KATE. The fog's breaking up. (*looks out*)

KITTY. I have a famous friend.

KATE. Swell.

KITTY. You've always known where you were going and how you'd get there.

KATE. That was grade school.

KITTY. High school too.

KATE. Well college is different. Not only harder but there're lots of people out there smarter. And they don't try and please everyone all the time. You were right, Kitty, I do want to be perfect. Remember when you said that?

KITTY. No.

KATE. Five years ago. Here at the lake. At first I was furious. Then I wanted to cry but I couldn't. Know why? I didn't feel enough.

KITTY. That's better than feeling too much, like me.

KATE. You're sensitive.

KITTY. I'm too easily hurt.

KATE. You know what I do when I start to feel something? I come on with my holier-than-thou superior look. Inside I'm dying to experience everything, but I never will because I act like I already have. Oh, Kitty, what if I die without ever feeling anything?

KITTY. Then you won't feel guilty all the time. That's what makes me feel like throwing myself in the lake.

KATE. Right now you wouldn't believe how guilty I feel. If I don't become the world's greatest writer my parents won't be proud of me and you'll be disappointed.

KITTY. But you'll make it. You've got talent.

KATE. I'm not as smart as you.

KITTY. But you're stronger.

KATE. No, Kitty, you are. You wouldn't let me change you.

KITTY. Did you want to?

KATE. I thought you wanted me to.

KITTY. All I want is to get married, be a good mother and have you as my friend.

KATE. You don't need me.

KITTY. You're my friend. My perfect friend. I love you.

KATE. The only thing perfect about me is that.

(*Fog horn blows.*)

KITTY. (*climbs ladder*) From up here you can see our boats.
Way out. Sailing together, neck and neck.

KATE. (*climbs ladder*) We're not across yet.

KITTY. But we're going to make it.

KATE. The trick is the journey.

KITTY. Isn't it hard to believe we're already twenty-one?

KATE. Seems like only minutes ago we were eleven.

KATE. (*extends hand*) Sometimes I wish we didn't have to get
any older.

KATE. (*takes Kitty's hand*) Wouldn't it be nice if now could be
always?

(*They hold hands as the light gets blinding bright before fading to
     black.*)

THE END

Intermission

A Play in One Act

by
Daniel Meltzer

INTERMISSION by Daniel Meltzer

1st Production May 25, 1982

Director	Robert Spera
Sets	Jonathan W. Sprouse
Lights	Jonathan W. Sprouse
Costumes	Diana S. Cain

CAST

THE DIRECTOR	JOEL HAMMER
THE WRITER	JOSEPH URLA
WOMAN #1	AMY THOMPSON
WOMAN #2	MELISSA WEIL
YOUNG WOMAN	PAMELA KORNHAAS
THE ACTRESS	SUSANNA BANKS

SETTING

A theatre lobby.

TIME

The present.

All programs and publicity materials for this play must carry the following notice:

COMMISSIONED AND FIRST PRODUCED BY ACTORS THEATRE OF LOUISVILLE

Intermission

A theatre lobby. The feeling of an intermission crowd. Murmur, laughter, drinking of wine, etc. Downstage area is brightly lit and U.S. *falls into shadow, suggestion of a bar area* U.S.. *Down left, a pretty YOUNG WOMAN stands, sipping white wine and looking through her playbill. She wears a simple, but slightly formal evening type dress. Down right, two men stand sipping wine and without playbills. THE WRITER wears a corduroy suit and turtle-neck shirt. He sips red wine. THE DIRECTOR wears a tuxedo and sips white wine.*

DIRECTOR. They're loving it. They are absolutely eating it up and dying for more. I haven't heard laughs like that since my first directing job.

WRITER. What was that?

DIRECTOR. *Macbeth.* (*pause*) You see the guy from the *Times*?

WRITER. I don't know. What does he look like?

DIRECTOR. What does he look like? He looks like he's gonna die of laughter.

WRITER. The second act's not that funny.

DIRECTOR. Doesn't have to be. They're gonna love it. They're with us, you can feel it.

WRITER. Let's take out the diaphragm joke.

DIRECTOR. Take it out?

WRITER. I'll give you the cut in the morning.

DIRECTOR. It's the biggest laugh in the show. It's the best line she's got.

WRITER. I don't like it.

DIRECTOR. You don't like it? You wrote it.

WRITER. It's a cheap joke.

DIRECTOR. It's the way she's doing it. I'll give her a note.

WRITER. It's out of character. We don't need it.

DIRECTOR. Leave it in. I'll work on it with her. It brought down the house. The guy from the *Times* nearly died.

WRITER. She's a flirt, she's not a whore. I'll give you the cut in the morning. We don't need it.

DIRECTOR. Okay, okay. Relax. In twelve hours you're gonna be famous. Guy from Paramount is sitting two rows in front of me, I thought he was gonna die.

WRITER. We've still got the second act.

DIRECTOR. The second act's beautiful. Don't worry about it. They're gonna cry like babies. Believe me.

WRITER. (*looking around*) Have you seen her?

DIRECTOR. Don't worry about her.

WRITER. Is she here?

DIRECTOR. Came in about ten minutes in.

WRITER. I thought I heard something. Who's she with?

DIRECTOR. What do you care?

WRITER. Who's she with?

DIRECTOR. You know. He's an asshole. Next one you write should be about *him*.

WRITER. (*looking around*) Where is she?

DIRECTOR. She's floatin' around somewhere. C'mon, I'll buy you another drink.

(*Takes him around the shoulder, leads him* U.S. *out of the light. Two women, dressed for an opening night, cross down into the light.*)

WOMAN #1. Did you see her?

WOMAN #2. How could you miss her? They always have to make an entrance. Always have to come in late.

WOMAN #1. Do you think she'll make a scene?

WOMAN #2. With him? Would you blame her?

WOMAN #1. He says it's not based on her.

WOMAN #2. Where did he say that?

WOMAN #1. Yesterday. In the "Arts and Leisure." Didn't you see it?

WOMAN #2. Jeffrey took it with him to the Coast.

WOMAN #1. Oh. He had an interview. You know. For the opening. And they asked him, naturally, because they were, you know, and because of what happened.

WOMAN #2. And he says it's not her.

WOMAN #1. That's what he says.

WOMAN #2. What do you expect him to say? Everybody knows it's her, anyway. Sure, he makes her a character, writes a play about her and then gives it to another actress. Men.

WOMAN #1. I heard she didn't want the part.

WOMAN #2. That's what *she* says. They're all such a bunch of phonies anyway. Carry on all over the place and then they want the whole world to love them. That's a nice bag, where did you get it?

WOMAN #1. Thank you. Saks.

WOMAN #2. It's a nice bag. You should get some nice shoes to go with it.

WOMAN #1. I did.

WOMAN #2. (*noticing*) Oh. Yes. Very nice. (*Pause. They sip their wine.*)

WOMAN #1. So . . . do you think it's a hit?

WOMAN #2. It better be.

WOMAN #1. How much did Jeffrey put in?

WOMAN #2. Don't ask.

WOMAN #1. He *is* very clever.

WOMAN #2. Clever. You shack up with a crazy actress and you write a play about it. What does it take to be clever?

WOMAN #1. Some of it's very funny.

WOMAN #2. The thing with the diaphragm was hysterical.

WOMAN #1. You thought so.

WOMAN #2. I thought I'd pee in my pants. How's the line at the ladies room?

WOMAN #1. *She's* in there.

WOMAN #2. She would be. Comes in late, right to the bathroom. You saw who she's with.

WOMAN #1. No. Who?

WOMAN #2. Who do you think? What's-his-name. You know. He owns all those . . . You know. His father is what's-his-name.

WOMAN #1. Oh. Him.

WOMAN #2. That's the one.

WOMAN #1. Do you think she'll make a scene?

WOMAN #2. She doesn't need him any more. That's for sure. Besides . . . I hear he's gay.

WOMAN #1. Who?

WOMAN #2. Him. You know. They all are. All the way back to Shakespeare. Please.

WOMAN #1. But what about with her? They were . . .

WOMAN #2. So, he's A.M.—F.M. That's even worse.

WOMAN #1. A.M.—F.M.? What's that?

WOMAN #2. Honestly. You really have to come into town more. Shhh. There he is. Watch how he walks.

(*The two women drift* D.R. *and mime conversation. THE WRITER crosses down into the light and stands near THE YOUNG WOMAN, who is still reading her Playbill. He looks to see what she is reading. She feels his presence and looks up. She smiles. He smiles back.*)

YOUNG WOMAN. I was reading about the author. He must be nervous as anything.

WRITER. I'm sure he is.

YOUNG WOMAN. Big Broadway opening. It's his first one, you know.

WRITER. Is it?

YOUNG WOMAN. Oh yes. Well, he's been writing for years and years, it says, but this is his first time on Broadway. Are you in the Theatre?

WRITER. I am at the moment.

YOUNG WOMAN. At the moment? Oh, I get it. I think everyone here is in the Theatre. Or something.

WRITER. And you?

YOUNG WOMAN. Me? Oh no. Not really. Well, my boss is, sort of. He's a backer. Do you know what that is?

WRITER. Yes, I believe so.

YOUNG WOMAN. Anyway, he couldn't come on account of he's out of town on business, so he let me have his ticket.

WRITER. That was very nice of him.

YOUNG WOMAN. Oh, I know. Isn't it exciting? All these famous people and everything. I think it's going to be a hit, don't you?

WRITER. You never can tell.

YOUNG WOMAN. Could I ask you something?

WRITER. Sure.

YOUNG WOMAN. Do you really think it's all that funny?

WRITER. What do you mean?

YOUNG WOMAN. Well, I mean I know it's a comedy and all that, but . . . Charlotte, is that her name?

WRITER. Carla.

YOUNG WOMAN. Carla. I'm terrible with names. Anyway, I don't know, I mean it *is* funny, but . . . I kind of feel sorry for her. Don't you?

WRITER. How do you mean?

YOUNG WOMAN. I mean, like, well . . . she's living with, you know, with the writer and I think he really cares about her, but she's just got this . . . this weakness. She's a woman who really wants to be loved and, well, he *does* love her but, well, you know writers, and he just doesn't show it . . . It's all inside and everything and now what's-his-name comes along with all his money and everything and I think she's just got this weakness. I hope she doesn't go off with him. Does she?

WRITER. Well, she already has.

YOUNG WOMAN. But that's just Act One. They'll get back together. Don't you think?

WRITER. Well, I . . .

YOUNG WOMAN. Don't tell me. Anyway, I guess I just don't find it as ha-ha funny as everybody else does. I mean, it *is* funny, but . . . Like, take that scene with the . . .

WRITER. Which scene?

YOUNG WOMAN. You know. I mean, first of all, she wouldn't be that careless about it. Unless she *wanted* him to know. Anyway, it made me uncomfortable. I mean, maybe she's a flirt and all that, but . . . she's not a tramp.

WRITER. You don't think so.

YOUNG WOMAN. Oh no. She just wants to be loved, that's all, and she keeps making all these dopey mistakes. Just like anyone. *I* can understand her. Can't you?

WRITER. I think so. But you don't think it's very funny.

YOUNG WOMAN. Oh, some of it's a scream. I mean, he's really clever the way he has them argue over the teeniest things all the time. Oh, God, is that ever true. He knows women, all right. Listen to me, going on like that and him probably standing right here where he can hear me. (*looks around*)

WRITER. Do you know what he looks like?

YOUNG WOMAN. I think he has a beard. Do you see him?

WRITER. No.

YOUNG WOMAN. Good. Once I get going . . .

WRITER. Do you . . . come to the theatre much?

YOUNG WOMAN. When I can afford it.

WRITER. Or on a date.

YOUNG WOMAN. Oh no. Pay my own way, that's me. Diana Dutch they call me. My name's Diane, but my friends call me Diana Dutch on account of that's the way I am. I like to pay my own way.

WRITER. Except for tonight.

YOUNG WOMAN. Well, this is different. I've never been to an opening night before. You?

WRITER. No.

YOUNG WOMAN. And anyway it was a free ticket. My boss had to go to California on business, only it isn't really business, if you know what I mean.

WRITER. What do you mean?

YOUNG WOMAN. There I go. You won't say anything. I'm sitting with his wife, too. She's got the other ticket. What do *you* do? If you don't mind my asking.

WRITER. I'm . . . a writer.

YOUNG WOMAN. I would've guessed lawyer, but I'm a terrible guesser. I'm a writer myself, sort of.

WRITER. What do you mean . . . sort of?

YOUNG WOMAN. Well, you know. Never had anything published, actually.

WRITER. What do you write?

YOUNG WOMAN. Short stories, mostly. And poems.

WRITER. What do you write about?

YOUNG WOMAN. Myself, mostly. And people I know. Nothing very exotic. I just like to write about very simple things. About what it's like inside. Do you know what I mean?

WRITER. Those are always the hardest.

YOUNG WOMAN. I don't know. It's the other part that's hard. Well, *you* know. Have you been published and everything?

WRITER. Some. Not very much.

YOUNG WOMAN. And you heard they're raising the postage rates again.

WRITER. Are they?

YOUNG WOMAN. And envelopes went up.

WRITER. You shouldn't give up.

YOUNG WOMAN. Don't worry about me. They'll find me over a typewriter. Sometimes it's better *not* being published, I think, anyway.

WRITER. What do you mean?

YOUNG WOMAN. Well, when you write about yourself and all, it's better you don't think about who's going to read it. Maybe I'll be published . . . (*She can't think of the word.*)

WRITER. Posthumously.

YOUNG WOMAN. Yeah. Then I don't care who reads it. (*A bell rings, summoning the audience for the second act.*) Well . . . curtain going up, as they say. It was . . . very nice talking to you.

WRITER. Listen . . .

YOUNG WOMAN. Yes?

WRITER. Would you . . . I'm going to a little party after the show, would you . . . Are you doing anything?

YOUNG WOMAN. Me?

WRITER. I think you might enjoy it.

YOUNG WOMAN. You're not married or anything, are you?
WRITER. No. I'm not married or anything.
YOUNG WOMAN. That's good. I was once, but that's a long story.

(*At this point, THE ACTRESS, a beautiful young woman in a provocative evening dress sweeps D.S. into the light towards THE WRITER, with THE DIRECTOR close behind, trying to hold her back.*)

DIRECTOR. Now, be cool, Charlotte, will ya? Don't do anything stupid.

YOUNG WOMAN. (*Recognizing THE ACTRESS*) Oh. Would you look who's there.

(*THE WRITER turns around and is face to face with THE ACTRESS.*)

WRITER. Charlotte.

(*There is a moment. A virtual tableau. THE WRITER and THE ACTRESS together, facing each other, C.S. THE YOUNG WOMAN just behind The WRITER, and THE DIRECTOR just behind THE ACTRESS. THE TWO WOMEN stop talking and watch from S.R. The murmur of voices that has been in the background fades and stops. It only lasts two or three seconds, and then . . .*)

WRITER. I'm glad you could make it.

(*THE ACTRESS throws her wine in The WRITER'S face. He stands stiffly.*)

ACTRESS. Faggot! (*THE TWO WOMEN gasp. THE YOUNG WOMAN puts her hand to her mouth.*)
DIRECTOR. Jesus Christ, Charlotte.
YOUNG WOMAN. Oh my.
WOMAN #2. Didn't I tell you? I told you he was. They all are. Come. (*She takes WOMAN #1 by the arm and leads her U.S. out of the light.*)
DIRECTOR. (*Leading THE ACTRESS off right by the arm.*)

Come on. What the hell did you want to do that for? Of all the goddamn stupid-ass . . .

(*THE WRITER and THE YOUNG WOMAN are alone,* c.s. *THE WRITER wipes his face with a handkerchief.*)

YOUNG WOMAN. That was a terrible thing to do.

WRITER. You'd better get back to your seat.

YOUNG WOMAN. I don't know what made me think you had a beard. I guess I thought all playwrights had beards. Shows how much I know. (*pause*) Aren't you going back in?

WRITER. I'll stand at the back. Listen . . . about that party.

YOUNG WOMAN. Oh, that's okay. I'm probably not dressed for it anyway. Besides, I've got lots to do. It was nice of you to ask me just the same.

WRITER. You're dressed fine. I just think I'll skip it.

YOUNG WOMAN. (*Takes handkerchief, folds it for him and arranges it in his jacket pocket.*) Skip it? Listen. You don't skip anything. This is your big night. You go to that party and you have yourself a time. And make an entrance. Tell you what. How about I let you buy me a drink after the show. I know, Diana Dutch and all that. Just this once. You can buy me a drink and then I'll owe you one and then you can make an entrance.

WRITER. I really . . .

YOUNG WOMAN. One drink. It won't kill ya.

DIRECTOR. (*smiles*) No. I guess it won't.

YOUNG WOMAN. I'll meet you right here, okay?

WRITER. Sure.

YOUNG WOMAN. I better get back to my seat or Mrs. What's-her-face'll have a fit. Listen . . . It's really a wonderful play.

WRITER. Thank you.

YOUNG WOMAN. Oh, I hear it starting. (*She quickly kisses him on the cheek, without even thinking, and dashes off* u.s.) See ya later.

(*THE WRITER reaches up and touches his cheek, looks around and turns and walks* u.s. *out of the light.*)

THE END

Love and Peace, Mary Jo

by
James Nicholson

LOVE AND PEACE, MARY JO by James Nicholson

1st Production December 18, 1981

Director. . . . . .Larry Deckel
Sets. . . . . Jonathan W. Sprouse
Lights. . . . . Pip Gordon

CAST

MARY JO. . . . . KATHERINE KLEKAS
PAUL. . . . . JACK YOUNG

All programs and publicity materials for this play must carry the
following notice:

COMMISSIONED AND FIRST PRODUCED BY ACTORS THEATRE OF LOUISVILLE

Love and Peace, Mary Jo

AT RISE: Darkness.

MARY JO. (*Voice over: TAPE*) It's not dying so much that bothers you. Somehow you get used to that. It's the sense of loneliness.

(*A telephone rings; lights up on PAUL's area of the stage*—S.L.)

PAUL. (*answering the phone*) Hello?
MARGE. (*voice on phone*) Sweetie, listen. Before you come, there's something you gotta know. Mary Jo has leukemia.

(*Crossfade to the central area of the stage—which will be utilized as the shared area. MARY JO is seated. She is frail—in truth, recovering from chemotherapy—and rigid in the manner of sick people who are doing their best not to be. PAUL walks into the area.*)

PAUL. Hi. (*pause*)
MARY JO. Long time no see. What have you been doing for the past three years?
PAUL. Not much. You?
MARY JO. I used to be busier. (*beat*) Do you still see people from FSU?
PAUL. When I can. Mainly we write.
MARY JO. I hardly write anyone any more. My opening paragraph tends to discourage open communication. (*beat*)
PAUL. How do you feel?
MARY JO. (*raising a finger*) Wrong question!
PAUL. Sorry.
MARY JO. Oh, I don't mind telling you. It's just that it's measured in degrees of bad and I've discovered that people lose interest real fast. (*a slight smile*) Better. The pain isn't bad. What bothers me most is I don't look like myself anymore. (*Crossfade to PAUL's area. He is speaking as he walks into the light.*)
PAUL. Dear Mary Jo,

Now that I've rediscovered you—guess what?—I'm going to write. You needn't feel compelled to respond; I'll write, anyway. School, so far, has been a real treat. One of my students, a mainstreamed refugee from the loony bin, has been mistaking me for a punching bag. The administration believes I should ignore him. Hard to do when the fist hits the . . . (*crossfade to MARY JO's area* — S.R.)

MARY JO. Yes, Paul Morrow, there really is a Mary Jo Walker alive and (thus) living in historic Alexandria, Virginia. Thank you for your letters which are just wonderful. To me, it is remarkable that you continue to write, considering only silence is offered in return. My apologies and, hopefully, this letter will serve to rebuke the silence. My thoughts are with you often, even if my letters are infrequent. Excuse any spelling and grammar errors. I'm a product of my generation. Love and peace, (*BLACKOUT*)

MARY JO. (*Voice over: TAPE*) At first, you withdraw into yourself and wish everything and everyone would go away. If you're lucky, that doesn't last long because it wastes precious time when you rediscover you're still alive.

(*Lights up on an empty hospital bed in an elevated area behind the central acting area.*)

MARY JO. (*Voice over: LIVE*) Hello from Baltimore! What am I doing here, you may ask (if you're smart, you won't!). I lost the remission in my Central Nervous System. There are several treatments for this. The one I am receiving is the injection of a drug in my spinal column. It is not the greatest of all things, but, considering the alternatives, it is not too bad. I'm not at the hospital, but at the Hilton (this is what your tax dollars are going for). It is probably the only time in my life I will have a chance to stay in one. And, until today, I made the most of it. (*crossfade to PAUL. He punctuates his speech by discarding the appropriate items.*)

PAUL. England was glorious. I wish I'd seen it. I had a Brit Rail pass for one week's unlimited travel and left London with great expectations. Unfortunately, somewhere between Coventry and Birmingham, the railway workers went on strike, I staggered back into London determined to recover at the National Theatre. Wrong. The stage hands were on strike. When I tried to come home, Air Canada and the French air traffic controllers were on strike. Separately. Somehow that meant my flight was delayed twelve hours and stopped in Toronto. Aren't you glad you weren't there to enjoy it all with me? (*Crossfade to MARY JO*)

MARY JO. BULLETIN — I'm back in remission.

(*Crossfade to the central area. They meet in it. They are watching the pandas at the National Zoo. MARY JO looks her healthiest.*)

PAUL. Pandas! We used to have pandas in Saint Louis. Now all we have is a panda cage filled with raccoons. It is definitely not the same.

MARY JO. How's Don? (*beat*)

PAUL. Good. He looked real good the last I saw him. Still lifting weights and strong as ever. And his hair's come back. He's real pleased about that.

MARY JO. He's so lucky it's Hodgkins. The recovery rate is phenomenal. Say hi to him for me.

PAUL. Sure. (*back to the pandas*) They let them play more in London. They have all sorts of things to climb and swing on there.

MARY JO. Here, they're preoccupied with protecting them. Not that they do such a good job of it. The last time I was here, I watched him eat a rat.

PAUL. He's supposed to be a vegetarian.

MARY JO. Tell it to the rat. He held the poor little thing by its tail and ate it like a popsicle. (*BLACKOUT*)

MARY JO. (*Voice over: TAPE*) Eventually, you learn to rely on others to supply strength when you need it. (*Lights up on PAUL.*)

MARY JO. (*Voice over: LIVE*) Happy Easter! Sorry about not writing before. For me, winter and depression are synonymous. Funny. My whole life seems to be watching—either plays, films or TV. A sad comment on me. Love and peace, Mary Jo. (I think) (*Crossfade to MARY JO*)

PAUL. (*Voice over: LIVE*) Guess what? I'm a godfather. Sort of. Tammy Aiello had a baby in class. Bet no one did that when you were in high school. And people wonder why teachers want more money. (*BLACKOUT*)

MARY JO. (*Voice over: TAPE*) You learn you need friends. And you learn who your friends really are. Some people do not react well to sickness, and fail you. Others surprise you with their loyalty.

(*Lights up on the central area. PAUL and MARY JO walk into it, talking. They are on the Mall. MARY JO, although seemingly healthy, is weaker than in the last scene.*)

PAUL. I love the Mall!

MARY JO. So do I, but I do my best not to act like a tourist while I'm on it.

PAUL. (*pointing*) What's that?

MARY JO. Still the Smithsonian.

PAUL. Really? Wanta go in?

MARY JO. (*sitting on a bench*) I think I'll sit this one out.

PAUL. (*joining her*) Right. Me, too. We'll sit for as long as I would've gawked. (*pause*)

MARY JO. Have you told Wendy about me?

PAUL. Shouldn't I have?

MARY JO. I wanted her to know. I just didn't want to tell her myself. I do want you to do me a favor, though.

PAUL. Sure. What?

MARY JO. Afterwards. I want you to let Wendy know. (*pause*)

PAUL. OK.

MARY JO. I don't think I have the courage to contact her, but I think of her a lot and I'd like her to know.

PAUL. Sure. (*Beat. He jumps up, then starts walking on his hands.*)

MARY JO. (*laughing*) What are you doing?

PAUL. Aren't you supposed to be crazy on the Mall?

MARY JO. Yes. But not like that.

PAUL. Why not?

MARY JO. Well, for one, you're getting dog dirt all over your hands. (*BLACKOUT. Lights up on the bed.*)

MARY JO. (*Voice over: LIVE*) Bad news. I lost the remission in my Central Nervous System. The doctors are still working, but I feel that I'm out of the woods. I think I set a record—12 spinal taps in 28 days. Excuse the handwriting, but I'm tiring. P.S. Keep me in your thoughts. I would appreciate it. (*Cross fade to PAUL*)

PAUL. Never fear. You are always in my thoughts. Please convey my sympathy to your spine. Mine would be rebelling by now. (*crossfade to MARY JO*)

MARY JO. The good news—I'm out of the woods. One more clear spinal tap and I'm back in remission. (*crossfade to the bed*)

MARY JO. (*Voice over: LIVE*) Just a short note to say I'm still here. I lost my remission yesterday, so it is back to the spinal taps. Will let you know how things go. (*Lights up on PAUL*)

PAUL. If it's any consolation, you've picked a good season to spend in bed. The roads around here are caked with snow and bordered with giant frosted lumps. Each lump contains someone's car. As the sidewalks have disappeared, people have taken

to walking their dogs on top of the lumps which really are cars.
Every so often, the roof of one gives way, causing extreme distress
to both dog and owner. (*Blackout on PAUL and the bed; lights up
on MARY JO.*)

MARY JO. Merry Christmas and Happy New Year. My medi-
cal status is still up in the air. I will get a clear tap and the next one
will have something in it. With time, it will straighten out.
(*BLACKOUT*)

MARY JO. (*Voice over: TAPE*) The strange thing is discovering
you can't do it alone. You really do need other people to help you
die.

(*Lights up on MARY JO seated at a table in the central area. She
shows the effects of the disease. PAUL walks in carrying two
beers. Beat.*)

PAUL. (*indicating a beer*) Can you have this?

MARY JO. Sure. I just can't have too many of them.

PAUL. (*fingering his mid-section*) That's a lesson I should have
learned a few years ago.

MARY JO. You look fine.

PAUL. So do you. To look at you, you'd never know your spine
is black and blue and full of holes.

MARY JO. Did you know I've been giving lectures on dying?

PAUL. No. To whom?

MARY JO. New patients. It's an experimental program. The
theory is you adjust better once you discover you're not alone.

PAUL. Does it work?

MARY JO. I think so. At any rate, the staff says I'm really
effective.

PAUL. That's terrific.

MARY JO. There is a problem.

PAUL. What?

MARY JO. They just asked me to tape my lecture.

PAUL. Real subtle, those medical social workers. (*pause*) Will
you?

MARY JO. I don't know. It seems so final. (*beat*) Besides, I think
I'm the wrong person to be giving advice. I'm becoming impossible. I'll argue about anything.

PAUL. I hadn't noticed.

MARY JO. You're not around enough to give me a chance. Ask
my parents; proximity brings out the worst in me. (*BLACKOUT*)

MARY JO. (*Voice over: TAPE*) When you become consistently

remiss in your dealings with others, it's a purely unscientific signal you're losing a remission. (*Lights up on the bed.*)

MARY JO. (*Voice over: LIVE*) I have been trying to write to you since Heaven knows when, but, now, I have no excuse. I'm in the hospital. The spinal taps were coming so fast that damage was occurring to my feet and legs. So the doctors suggested a reservoir placed in my head which they could treat directly. I now resemble the woman in Star Trek, but am nowhere as attractive! (*crossfade to PAUL*)

PAUL. She may look better with a bald head, but I bet you have more personality. Tammy Aiello brought the baby back to school today for a visit and to thank me for passing her so she could graduate. I told her she deserved a little extra credit for originality. (*crossfade to MARY JO*)

MARY JO. Yes, I'm still here! March was a month of going to Baltimore three times a week. The rest of the month was spent recovering from these visits to Baltimore. Two paragraphs and I've run out of news. God — what a boring life! I think I will close and, now, at least, you know I'm still here and your letters don't come to a vacant house (only to a vacant mind). (*crossfade to PAUL*)

PAUL. You should be speaking of vacant minds? I'll have you know I have taught some of the most vacant minds in the country and yours cannot compare. Try to be patient. Your body needs time to recover from all the shocks and indignities it's received. I know. Mine's still trying to recover from a mishap involving my left thumb, a very sharp knife and a rock hard bagel. (*crossfade to the bed*)

MARY JO. (*Voice over: LIVE*) This may be a very short letter, but I have to let you know how much your letters have meant to me. The leukemia is on the move and I'm in the middle of a series of radiation on the brain and spinal cord. It will just take time and effort. Excuse the shortness of this note, but you are in my thoughts often. It is only my spelling, grammar and effort that are lacking. (*Lights up on PAUL.*)

PAUL. Your spelling and grammar are just fine (my students should do as well) and your effort puts the rest of us to shame. Do try to have a Merry Christmas and a (*The phone rings; he answers it.*) Hello?

MARGE. (*Voice on phone*) Paul? (*BLACKOUT on the bed.*) I have bad news, sweetie. Mary Jo died this afternoon. (*BLACKOUT on PAUL.*)

MARY JO. (*Voice over: TAPE*) Your will to live seems to come from the feeling of being loved and cared for by others. And, possibly, it's the knowledge that you have made a lasting impression on those you love which makes the struggle seem worthwhile. Take care. Love and peace, Mary Jo.

THE END

Marred Bliss

by
Mark O'Donnell

MARRED BLISS by Mark O'Donnell

First Production May 26, 1987

Director...................................Larry Deckel
Sets.......................................Paul Owen
Lights.....................................Cliff Berek
Costumes...................................Kevin McLeod

CAST

JANE.......................................DENISE CAMPION
DINK.......................................NICK PHELPS
JEERY......................................DAVID BEACH
ALAS.......................................AMANDA RAMBO

SETTING

A porch.

All programs and publicity material for this play must carry the following notice:

COMMISSIONED AND FIRST PRODUCED BY ACTORS THEATRE OF LOUISVILLE

Marred Bliss

SCENE: The front porch of JANE's family home.
AT RISE: JANE arranges roses in a vase. DINK sits on the glider,
reading the paper or just enjoying the evening. It's a typical
midwestern scene. JANE is a pretty, prissy, inhibited young
woman, wearing starched, modest clothes. DINK is a regular
lug who's been talked into marriage but is willing to turn
himself over to it.

JANE. Darkling?

DINK. (*looking up from his paper*) What is it . . . Dulling?

JANE. I thought we'd have ruses for the centerpieces. For us,
and for all the guest tables. Ruses *are* traditional.

DINK. Ruses it is. (*He returns to his reading.*)

JANE. (*after a restless pause*) Oh honey, just *sink*!

DINK. What do you want me to sink about?

JANE. In less than forty eight horrors, you and I will be moan
and woof! (*grins*) Isn't it amassing?

DINK. It *is* amassing. (*lowers his paper thoughtfully*) So much
has harpooned in just a few thief years!

JANE. It steams like only yesterday that you were the noise next
door.

DINK. And you were that feckless-faced cod sitting up in the
old ache tree!

JANE. And now we're encaged! I can hardly wait till we're
marred!

DINK. Oh, Hiney! (*makes to enfold her in his arms*)

JANE. Now, now! I'm sure the tame will pass quickly till our
hiney-moon! (*eases out of his grasp*) I'll go get you some of that
nice saltpeter taffy that Smother brought back from A Frantic
City. (*JEERY, a sexy, slouching sailor, appears at one corner of
the stage.*)

JEERY. Hello? . . . Any him at home? (*He carries a tiny
bouquet.*)

JANE. Oh my gash! It's Jeery, my old toyfriend!

DINK. Jeery! That bump! What's *he* brewing here?

JANE. Oh, Dueling! Try to control your tamper! I'm sure he
means no charm! Don't do anything you might regress! (*JEERY
approaches.*)

JEERY. Hollow!—Revised to see me?

JANE. Hollow, Jeery.

DINK. Hollow. (*pause*)

JEERY. I'm completely beware that I'm out of police here. But—(*looks to JANE*)—for old climb's sake—Jane—I brought you this little bunch of foul airs. A token of my excess steam. Lots of lack to you. And much lack to you too, Dink.

JANE. (*unsurely*) Wail . . . (*decides to accept the flowers*) Spank you, Jeery.

DINK. Spank you very much.

JEERY. My shit is at rancor in the harbor, and they gave me whore leave. I heard you were engorged, and I just wanted to slop by and pave my regrets.

JANE. (*uncomfortably*) Well, blank you!

DINK. Blank you very much.

JANE. (*uneasy with this stand-off*) I think you two have already messed, haven't you?

JEERY. Oh, we've thrown each other for years!

DINK. We went to the same cruel . . . Till Jeery dripped out to join the Nervy.

JANE. Of course, I remainder all that now! (*She is eager to lessen the awkwardness.*) Um—Do you haunt to sit down?

JEERY. Well, only for a menace. (*He sits with them on the glider.*) I'm hooded over to Pain Street. There's a big trance at the Social Tub. I'll probably go and chick it out. (*awkward silence as they sit on the crowded glider*) Wail, wail, wail . . . So when do you two tie the net?

JANE. The day after temerity!

JEERY. That soon?

DINK. (*curtly*) We've been enraged for over a year.

JEERY. Well, concatenations!

DINK. Rank you very much . . . (*tense pause*). . . Jeery, it's getting awfully lout! You don't want to miss the trance! (*From the other entrance comes ALAS, a provocatively dressed woman with elaborate hair and a loose manner.*)

ALAS. Hell's own? Hell's own?

JANE. (*aside*) Oh no! Is that who I slink it is? Why won't she let us align? (*ALAS advances.*)

ALAS. Hell's own, every burden! Hell's own, Dink! . . .

DINK. (*uncomfortable but heated*) Hell's own, Alas! . . . Fantasy seething you here!

JANE. (*tartly*) I thought you'd be at the social tub trance, Alas. Aren't you on the degradation committee?

ALAS. (*offers a gift-wrapped bottle*) I may stoop by there later. I sinfully wanted to winch you both all the beast. Let icons be icons. Here's a battle of damn-pain for you — I hype you enjoy it.

JANE. (*suspicious*) How sweat of you. (*takes bottle, puts it aside*) You know Jeery, don't you, Alas?

ALAS. Yes, we mated years ago. How's the Nervy, Jeery?

JEERY. Great! I was born to be a soiler. (*Another awkward silence as they regard her.*)

DINK. (*To ALAS:*) Um — Would you like to hit with us, Alas? Jane, you don't grind if Alas hits with us, do you?

JANE. Well, the glider's getting awfully clouded!

ALAS. (*airily*) I'll just loin against the railing! (*She poses against the pillar seductively.*)

DINK. No, here, have my seed! (*stands*)

JANE. Dallying! (*pulls him back into his seat*) I think she'd rather remain stunning!

DINK. (*getting agitated*) Jeery, you could awful her *your* seat! Don't they teach you manners in the Harmed Surfaces? (*JEERY bristles.*)

JANE. (*to avoid a scene*) Look, qualm down! Maybe we should admit this is an awkward saturation! I have complete face in you, Dink — But I think it's in power taste for your old street-part to come around so soon before our welding!

ALAS. (*offended*) I can't bereave this! There's no reason to be sub-species, Jane!

JANE. (*affronted*) No?

ALAS. This is a Good Wall visit, that's all! You're just high-stung!

DINK. (*chiming in his objections*) And what about Jeery here! I don't luck having him luring at you!

JEERY. (*contemptuously*) Oh, relapse, Dink! Afraid she'll realize her Must-Ache before the Sorrow-Money? (*To ALAS:*) He's in debt, it's a mortgage of convenience!

JANE. (*frightened by this sudden passion*) Toys, please! Clam yourself! (*Earnestly, to DINK:*) Dink, don't drought yourself this way! Where's the strong, stabled man I'm taking to the halter? You know I lug you, I'll always lug you. (*puts her arms around him maternally*) I want ours to be a beautiful cremation-trip. But it has to be based on *truss*. (*hugs him even more suffocatingly, and not erotically*) I want to be able to *truss* you.

DINK. (*too independently to suit Jane*) All I did was offer Alas my seed. You act like I rammed off with her!

JANE. (*feels dressed down before company*) Well, maybe you'd rather ram off with her! She's been trying to reduce you since she got here!

ALAS. (*angry*) Don't spike like that to me! I bitter go.

JANE. (*her insecurity making her hysterical*) Stew where you are, you're the claws of this! You *slot*!

ALAS. (*sneering at JANE*) —What a little squirrel! I have nothing but potty for you!

(*The women suddenly slap each other; the men must intervene.*)

JEERY. (*restraining ALAS*) The whole tissue is ridiculous! Fighting over a man who's in doubt up to his ears!

DINK. At least I'm not diddled with funereal disease, you bellow-jellied bull-bottomed sin of the beach!

JEERY. You sod-damned cowbird!

(*The men fight; now the women must intervene.*)

ALAS. Boys! Stomp it! Stomp it this minute!

(*There is momentary silence as they all recover from their wounds.*)

JANE. *Why are we having such trouble trying to communicate?*

DINK. (*taking the lead*) . . . Look. Alas . . . I heave nothing but harpy memories of our time together. I depreciate your good winces, but Jane and I are to be marred, and that's that. (*He looks to Jane to match his definitive renunciation.*)

JANE. (*taking Jeery's hand briefly*) And. . . Jeery . . . I leave you very much. You know that. But that's all winter under the fridge. (*turns to ALAS*) Alas, I'm sorry I lost my torpor.

ALAS. (*with dignity*) I understand. And I axe-up your apology. Anyway, I'm getting marred myself. To Henry Silverstone.

JANE. (*impressed*) The banker! But he's rather old for you, isn't he?

ALAS. Luckily, he's in very good wealth. (*A car horn honks from offstage.*) There's my chauffeured limbo now. I'd better get gilding. Conglomerations, and gall the best! . . . Goad bye!

DINK. (*feeling bested*) Bile!

JANE. (*feeling outdone*) Bile!

(*ALAS Exits. JEERY now feels superfluous.*)

JEERY. Her own limbo! . . . Well, I guess I should leave you two lifeboats alone!

JANE. Thanks for the foul airs, Jeery! Enjoy the trance!

JEERY. Maybe I'll meet *my* future broad!

DINK. (*as if to a buddy*) That's the right platitude!

JEERY. So long! Have a lot of skids!

DINK. Bile!

JANE. Bile! (*JEERY goes*) He's a good spore, isn't he?

DINK. (*reluctantly*) I gas so.

JANE. (*hugging him consolingly*) But you're the *uphill* of my eye!

DINK. Oh, hiney! (*He holds and tries to kiss her, but she resists him.*) Oh come on! Ploys? Pretty ploys? (*She relents and gives him a peck, then quickly raises ALAS' gift bottle between them.*)

JANE. Oh look! A vintage battle of damn pain! Let's celibate! (*She pops it open and pours some of it into two empty lemonade glasses on the porch table. She raises her glass.*) I love it when those little troubles get up your nose! — Here, let's test each other! (*they toast*) To *ice*!

DINK. To *ass*! (*they drink*)

JANE. Oh, galling! Our life together is going to be *blitz*!

BLACKOUT

THE END

Subterranean Homesick Blues Again

by
Dennis Reardon

SUBTERRANEAN HOMESICK BLUES AGAIN
by Dennis Reardon

1st production May 25, 1983

Director. . . . . K. Wynne West
Sets. . . . . .Paul Owen
Lights. . . . . Tracy Dedrickson
Costumes. . . . . Ginger Blake

CAST

TOUR GUIDE. . . . . .BRUCE WIELAND
NAOMI. . . . . ANNETTE HILLMAN
SHERMAN. . . . . MARK LOFTIS
MICK. . . . . SCOTT PHELPS
KATHY. . . . . AMY APPLEBY

SETTING

A cave.

All programs and publicity material for this play must carry the
following notice:

COMMISSIONED AND FIRST PRODUCED BY ACTORS
THEATRE OF LOUISVILLE

Subterranean Homesick
Blues Again

SCENE: This playlet takes place within a cave. It could conceivably be lit with five flashlights, though special effects lighting would help.

AT RISE: From a BLACKOUT, harsh underlighting on the face of the TOUR GUIDE. He speaks rather softly but precisely. He's a handsome 19 year old; his manner is pleasant and more polished than his years would indicate. Still, there is a slight mechanical quality to him — he's only doing his job.

TOUR GUIDE. Good afternoon. Welcome to the Caverns. Over the next few minutes you will be descending by elevator and stairs a distance of some fifteen hundred feet into the bowels of the earth. (*he smiles*) The temperature throughout the Caverns is a constant 54 degrees. The Caverns maintain this temperature all year round, come rain, snow, or heat of summer. If at any point you have any questions, please don't hesitate to ask. Is everybody in? Good. Going Doowwwnnn . . . (*Brief BLACKOUT, then . . . underlight* Tour Guide.) Welcome to the first landing. Behold the majestic skeleton of your Mother Earth.

(*Lights up on two tourist couples, aged variously from 19 to 25: they are MICK & KATHY and NAOMI & SHERMAN, all friends of long-standing. They are all rubber-necking the scene around them. Only NAOMI is remotely impressed, and she excessively so.*)

NAOMI. Oh mah Gaawwddd . . .

SHERMAN. Oh your god what?

NAOMI. It's awesome, utterly stupefying!

SHERMAN. C'mon . . . it looks like the inside of a cement plant. (*MICK & KATHY laugh.*)

MICK. It ain't Carlsbad Caverns, that's for sure.

KATHY. I'm cold.

NAOMI. You *people*! What does it take to *impress* you? An earthquake? A tornado? A vol*ca*no?

MICK. Tornado would do it for me, Sherm, how 'bout you?

SHERMAN. Gimme a volcano. With lots of hot, flowing lava . . .

KATHY. Oh, you guys . . .

TOUR GUIDE. This chamber was channeled out over a period of 200,000 years. We call it the Great Cathedral.

MICK. Looks like an airplane hangar.

TOUR GUIDE. In the corner a limestone formation some forty feet high called God's Organ. (*All the tourists burst out laughing.*)

KATHY. Oh you guy-yize! That's *not* what the poor boy *meant*! (*The TOUR GUIDE stares neutrally at them*) Is it?

SHERMAN. What's it look like to you, Naomi? A giant skin flute? (*To MICK:*) That's her specialty.

NAOMI. (*angry*) That's *not* funny!

KATHY. Yeah, grow up, you guys.

TOUR GUIDE. Off to either side, you will see lights illuminating a series of cul-de-sacs — or so the management would have you believe. Supposedly they've all been thoroughly investigated and none of them descend more than twenty-five feet. I can personally assure you that is a lie. This cave is far more extensive than the public is led to believe. Shall we proceed?

SHERMAN. Hey, for seven bucks a pop, you better show us *all* of it!

MICK. (*To KATHY, but meaning to be overheard:*) Is he bitching about money again? Who bought lunch, tell me that?

KATHY. Isn't anybody else *cold*? (*NAOMI suddenly shrieks; when she has everyone's attention:*)

NAOMI. Good GOD! I feel so *mired* in you all! (*Silence. All stare at her.*)

SHERMAN. Do you have any idea how pretentious that sounds?

(*BLACKOUT. Underlight Tour Guide; side lighting on Tourists.*)

TOUR GUIDE. The Second Level. Note the interesting cascade formation set off by the pink lighting. The current management sees fit to call this feature The Hippie's Hairdo. (*MICK, KATHY, and SHERMAN laugh. NAOMI is still exasperated, angry.*)

NAOMI. How *recherché*.

TOUR GUIDE. I prefer its original name, The Head of Medusa.

NAOMI. Much more appropriate. (*explaining to the others*) Medusa had a headful of snakes, and her gaze turned men into stone.

SHERMAN. Hey Babe, she had nothing on you.

MICK. (*laughing*) Stone me, Naomi.

NAOMI. Do you assholes really want to go at it? Right down

here in front of this innocent bystander? (*indicating GUIDE*)
Cause I'm ready.

KATHY. Now honey, the boys were just pulling your leg a bit.
Relax, o.k.? (*NAOMI glares at them all.*)

TOUR GUIDE. Look folks, I don't think you're in the spirit of
this thing. Why don't we call it a day?

SHERMAN. You trying to gyp us, you lazy bastard?

MICK. Just do your rap, kid. We're listenin'.

KATHY. Oh yes, please do go on. It's all so interesting, about
the rocks and all. (*admonishing the others*) Now I think we should
all behave just a *little bit better.* Don't you?

MICK. Yes, Mother.

TOUR GUIDE. All right. Let's try it again. Ahead and to your
right is perhaps the most famous feature of the Caverns, the
Bridal Chamber.

KATHY. Oh Naomi, for heaven's sake, look there on the floor
—a heart carved out of stone!

NAOMI. Sooo tacky.

TOUR GUIDE. Every year as many as thirty couples get married
right here, right over that stone heart. Of course a lot of those folks
are so ugly their parents make 'em go underground. (*No laugh
from the Tourists, though NAOMI manages a snicker.*)

MICK. Did the guy tell a joke? (*SHERMAN shrugs and
snickers.*)

TOUR GUIDE. That was actually number three in my routine,
but I skipped the first two because you people were doing so well
yourselves. (*NAOMI & KATHY laugh; the men don't.*)

SHERMAN. How much money did this joint gross last year?

TOUR GUIDE. A lot more than you did, I'm sure. (*He walks off.
The tourists follow.*)

SHERMAN. Cheeky bastard, isn't he?

(*BLACKOUT. Underlighting on TOUR GUIDE.*)

TOUR GUIDE. The Third Level. We are now deep within the
Earth. Fifteen hundred feet above us the sun is shining and birds
are singing. Here, no birds sing. There are no fresh breezes to cool
you on a warm summer day. Here there is no warmth, and the
sun never, ever, shines. (*The tourists no longer joke around.*)

KATHY. Mick, he's making me feel so much *colder.* (*MICK,
irritated, takes off his sweater and thrusts it at her.*) No, honey, I
wouldn't want you catching cold on my account.

MICK. Kathy, take it and shut up, will ya? I'm sick of your whining. (*She poutingly pulls the sweater on. The tourists trudge along.*)

TOUR GUIDE. We are within the Rock of Ages. Don't be afraid to touch the stone. Run your hands over it. (*NAOMI and, more tentatively, KATHY mime the action. Men sullenly refuse.*) There are dead thir.gs in those walls. (*The women pull back.*) A mountain of corpses.

NAOMI. Fossils. You mean fossils, don't you?

TOUR GUIDE. The carcasses of millennia. At the very top, still closest to the sun, the debris of man. Broken pots. The skeletons of some prehistoric Indians. Going deeper, getting older, the years receding like clouds. The pelvis of a three foot ancestor to the gray rat. Giant wooly elephants. Birds' feet in amber. The intact skeleton of a sixty foot viper! Things were grander then, and look! The jawbone of the Thunder Lizard, Tyrannosaurus Rex! Death was never so rapacious, so ravening, not until the coming of man. (*pointing upward*) Now look high above you, as far into the darkness as you can. You are staring up through solid time three and one half billion years to the beautiful dark living soil fifteen hundred feet above. And what do you see? Billions of your brothers and sisters floating on the surface of the centuries, like an oil slick upon the face of the deep. (*He smiles.*) Like scum on a Dead Sea. (*The tourists are somewhat cowed by him now. He suddenly gestures them to an even deeper silence.*) Don't breathe, just listen. (*pause*) Can you hear it? The whispering? Water. An underground river. There, off in the blackness to your right, and ten feet below. We call it the River Styx. (*He smiles.*) We've reserved a boat for you.

(*BLACKOUT. In dim light, tinged red, seated in chairs behind a cut-out of a flat-bottomed boat, sit the tourists. Behind and above them, grim as a god, the TOUR GUIDE poles the boat along the Styx. The tourists are somber.*)

TOUR GUIDE. You may think you move now through a dead world. This is not precisely true. Where our floodlights strike water running over the rock, there is algae. And in the upper reaches of the Caverns there are bats. Finally, in the water beneath you there are little colorless blind fish swimming around in the blackness.

NAOMI. (*nervously*) And what do these poor little fish find to eat?

TOUR GUIDE. No one is sure. My personal opinion is that they feed on venial sins. (*He poles on for a few moments until NAOMI's face fills with horror.*)

NAOMI. Oh my God. We've died and gone to Hell.

SHERMAN. Naomi, don't have another nervous breakdown on me, please?

MICK. Not down here, Naomi, come on, now . . .

KATHY. It's fun! Don't you think it's fun, Mick? Huh?

TOUR GUIDE. At this point many of our clients are interested to learn that we have long since left behind the Public Access portion of the Caverns.

SHERMAN. What? What's he saying?

TOUR GUIDE. Look there, off to your left. You see the little light? That's my home. Very peaceful.

NAOMI. Oh, my gaawwdd. . . .

MICK. I think this has gone far enough, guy.

TOUR GUIDE. Charon. The name is Charon.

MICK. I don't want to go no farther than anybody else, you understand? I'm sick of this tour. Turn it around and take us back. (*No response from TOUR GUIDE. He continues to pole gently.*)

SHERMAN. What is this, part of your routine? Gag number four, right? Look, enough's enough! You're scaring the wives!

TOUR GUIDE. Don't be impatient. We're almost there. Can you see? The Island of the Contentious.

KATHY. (*whispering, horrified*) Look at all those people . . .

NAOMI. They stare at us. Only their eyes move.

MICK. Are they dead? Are we?

TOUR GUIDE. When they first arrived, they made lots of noise and jumped around and hit each other. That's what you'll do, too. For a while. It doesn't last long. Eventually the silence will overcome your wrath. You will become like the darkness engulfing you. Silent. Unmoved. (*a beat, then*) Here we are. Let me help the ladies off.

KATHY. I don't want to go.

TOUR GUIDE. Of course you do. This is home now. (*calling out into the darkness*) Halloo! Another load of little blind fish! (*He helps the ladies out.*)

MICK. Kathy, don't! Get back in!

TOUR GUIDE. Please, let's be men about this, shall we? The other way gets so messy. (*Sound: A deep, snurfling animal noise, like a bull or a big dog.*)

SHERMAN. What is that? What is that sound?

MICK. Ooh, nooo . . .

TOUR GUIDE. Stay, Cerberus! If you just get out of the boat, he won't hurt you.

(*The men get out. TOUR GUIDE begins to pole back the other direction, talking informatively and amiably to them as he recedes.*)

TOUR GUIDE. If at first you feel chilled, it might help you to realize that beneath your feet, surprisingly near, is a sphere of liquid fire, called by man the Athenosphere. Think of it as a world of lava. Or, if it suits you, think of it as Hell. You feel warmer already, don't you? (*He poles on a bit more.*) Don't worry, you're not destined for the flames. Your sins are not that profound. No, your fate is simply to dwell in eternal Darkness. Do you feel it now? The Blackness engulfing you as we part? A deeper blackness than any of your nights upon the earth. (*The tourists can be seen making classic gestures of entreaty and penitence, imploring the TOUR GUIDE to return with them.*) Here you will soon be at peace. Your eyes will grow accustomed to the restful absence of color. You will quickly forget that you *have* eyes . . . or ears, or minds. The turbulence and confusion of your days beneath the sun are ended. You are the night. Fare thee well, Shades.

(*A last brief BLACKOUT. Then lights up quickly on the cast assembled. Then out.*)

THE END

The Field

by
Robert Spera

THE FIELD by Robert Spera

1st Production December 22, 1982

Director.	Larry Deckel
Sets.	Paul Owen
Lights.	Tracy Dedrickson
Costumes.	Ginger Blake

CAST

JAKE.	ROBERT MORAN
MICKEY.	SHAWN DOUGHERTY

SETTING

A field.

All programs and publicity material for this play must carry the following notice:

COMMISSIONED AND FIRST PRODUCED BY ACTORS
THEATRE OF LOUISVILLE

The Field

AT RISE: Lights come up on two young men
  Both are standing perfectly still in a grass
  ahead and laughing hysterically. It is late
  the action that they are working their way a

JAKE. (*laughing*). . . . a bowling ball you cou
to. . . .

MICKEY. (*laughing*). . . . yeah, a bowling ball you could eat if
you had to. . . .

JAKE. I can't believe it. . . . a bowling ball you could (*laughter
is now out of control*) eat if you had to. . . .

MICKEY. Right?

JAKE. Oh, I hurt. I'm going to blow a gasket. . . . a bowling
ball you . . .

MICKEY. You like that?

JAKE. No. (*This answer sends them into another spasm of
laughter that continues for a few moments and then begins to
slowly dissolve into a serious tone.*)

MICKEY. Too much, right?

JAKE. Yeah. (*long pause*)

MICKEY. (*serious*) O.K., ready.

JAKE. OK, I got one.

MICKEY. O.K.

JAKE. Wait I got a better one.

MICKEY. O.K.

JAKE. (*serious*) Why did the elephant step on the
marshmallow?

MICKEY. (*serious, he prepares to take a step*) Why did the
elephant step on the marshmallow?

JAKE. Easy, Mickey. Go easy, Mickey.

MICKEY. (*Extremely tense, he takes two or three deep breaths.*)
Easy, I'm going. (*Lets out a low grunt as he slowly lifts his foot and
gently places it in front of him.*)

JAKE. (*proud*)You son of a bitch.

MICKEY. You owe me. Hit me. Why did the fucking elephant
step on the marshmallow?

JAKE. So he wouldn't fall in the hot chocolate. (*eruption of
hysterical laughter*)

MICKEY. (*laughing*) So he wouldn't fall in the hot chocolate.

195

ᴇ. (*laughing*) My all-time favorite.

ᴍɪᴄᴋᴇʏ. Priceless. Absolutely priceless.

Jᴀᴋᴇ. Yeah.

Mɪᴄᴋᴇʏ. Yeah. (*Once again laughter begins to fade and trail off into a serious tone as they anticipate the next step. Long pause*)

Jᴀᴋᴇ. I know. I'm ready.

Mɪᴄᴋᴇʏ. You OK?

Jᴀᴋᴇ. Asshole lieutenant.

Mɪᴄᴋᴇʏ. Forget about it.

Jᴀᴋᴇ. You kidding me or what?

Mɪᴄᴋᴇʏ. Forget about it.

Jᴀᴋᴇ. There was this lieutenant over with charley company got wasted by his own squad for a lot less.

Mɪᴄᴋᴇʏ. I know.

Jᴀᴋᴇ. No shit. His squad was out on a lurp for three days. No sleep, humping their asses uphill for three days. Two guys got greased on a wire. LT gets them back and has them pull latrine duty. Talk about insensitive, right? Two weeks later, courtesy of that jerk-off they walk into a firefight with some regulars and during the course of events someone *accidentally* puts a round into the old man.

Mɪᴄᴋᴇʏ. Yeah.

Jᴀᴋᴇ. Sorry-ass sucker deserved it.

Mɪᴄᴋᴇʏ. Yeah.

Jᴀᴋᴇ. And the gem we got waltzes us right in here. You see him with the map? Sad-ass sucker couldn't figure which way was up. He be turning the map this way, that way, scratching his head saying uh huh, uh huh. I mean three weeks ago he was running through some woods in Virginia shooting red dye at people and I'm supposed to take orders from him?

Mɪᴄᴋᴇʏ. You done?

Jᴀᴋᴇ. Yeah. Sorry.

Mɪᴄᴋᴇʏ. Sure?

Jᴀᴋᴇ. Come on, don't bust my chops. (*pause*)

Mɪᴄᴋᴇʏ. (*serious*) What is the brown goo between an elephant's toes?

Jᴀᴋᴇ. (*serious*)What is the brown goo between. . . .

Mɪᴄᴋᴇʏ. (*cuts him off*) Right, what is the brown goo between an elephant's toes?

Jᴀᴋᴇ. (*prepares to take a step*) What is the brown goo between an elephant's toes?

MICKEY. Easy, Jake. Come on baby. Come on Jake. Easy, baby.

JAKE. Easy. I'm going. I'm going. (*Extremely tense, JAKE has much less confidence than MICKEY when moving. He takes seven or eight deep breaths, lets out a wild scream and takes a step forward.*) AAAAAAAAAAAHHHHHHHHKKK! No sweat right? No sweat. No clicks, right? Mickey right? You didn't hear any clicks, right? Mickey did you hear a click or what? Mickey?

MICKEY. (*laughing*) Right, no clicks, Jake.

JAKE. Right. No sweat. No sweat. Did you see me? Hit me. What is the brown goo between an elephant's toes?

MICKEY. Slow running natives. (*eruption of laughter*)

JAKE. Slow running natives. . . .

MICKEY. Yeah, slow running natives.

JAKE. I swear I'm gonna bust.

MICKEY. Primo, huh, Jakey.

JAKE. From now on call me "no-clicks Jakey".

MICKEY. (*just laughs*) No clicks. Who said clicks? It won't sound like a click.

JAKE. What the hell do you mean it won't sound like a click? It'll be a click, you said that. A click.

MICKEY. I said something *like* a click.

JAKE. What do you mean something *like* a click? Come on, Mickey. Don't screw around. Is it a click or isn't it?

MICKEY. It's more like a snap than a click.

JAKE. What do you mean? What's the difference?

MICKEY. Forget about it.

JAKE. I can't forget about it. How will I know if I hit one?

MICKEY. If you're not sure, lift your leg. If you didn't hit one, your leg will still be there.

JAKE. Hysterical. Come on, Mickey, you kidding or what? Mickey? I'm serious. Don't play around. Will it sound like a click or not?

MICKEY. (*breaks out laughing*) Yes, it will sound like a click, you baby. (*imitating JAKE:*) Come on Mickey, don't play around. I'm serious. You baby.

JAKE. I just wanted to know.

MICKEY. Right.

JAKE. It is a click then, right?

MICKEY. Jesus, leave me alone. Yes, it's a click.

JAKE. Good. That's all I wanted to know.

MICKEY. It doesn't make a difference anyway.

JAKE. I don't want to hear about it.

MICKEY. Back in March, guy named Ace tripped one over on Hill 34. We had to go over and collect what was left of the poor bastard. Brought him back in a shoe box.

JAKE. Terrific!

MICKEY. Hey. While I was looking for him, I ran across his boot. I picked it up and his frigging foot was still inside. I mean his leg, cut right off at the top of his boot.

JAKE. Shit.

MICKEY. Hey. (*long pause*)

JAKE. Mickey, this stuff is getting real old real fast.

MICKEY. Come on, let's go.

JAKE. No. No more.

MICKEY. What? You're planning on setting up house here?

JAKE. You want to go, you go.

MICKEY. I can't, you gotta give me a joke.

JAKE. I don't know anymore.

MICKEY. Make one up.

JAKE. You make one up.

MICKEY. Fuck it then. (*pause*) Hey, you wouldn't mind if I looked up your chick when I get back to the world, would you?

JAKE. Go to hell.

MICKEY. Well, shit, somebody's going to get into her, might as well be your best buddy.

JAKE. Lay off that shit, Mick.

MICKEY. Then get your ass in gear.

JAKE. Yeah, yeah, yeah.

MICKEY. Yeah, yeah, yeah. Right, now come on, give me a joke.

JAKE. I said I don't know anymore.

MICKEY. Alright, alright. How about a song? You know any songs?

JAKE. No. Oh wait, I got one. I can't remember the title.

MICKEY. How does it go?

JAKE. (*sings*) A hundred bottles of beer on the wall, a hundred bottles of beer. . . .

MICKEY. That's the name of it.

JAKE. Right, so what do we do with it?

MICKEY. OK, let's say you start singing, right? Then when you get to the part where the number changes, you stop singing and I take a step and I continue singing the next verse and we go on from there. How about it?

JAKE. Then we keep switching on and off?

MICKEY. Yeah.

JAKE. We're going to look like the frigging Rockettes.

MICKEY. Yeah, you start.

JAKE. (*starts singing, slow and serious*) A hundred bottles of beer on the wall, a hundred bottles of beer. If one of these bottles should happen to fall . . .

MICKEY. (*takes a deep breath, steps and sings*) Ninety-nine bottles of beer on the wall. (*He smiles and continues singing a bit quicker.*) Ninety-nine bottles of beer on the wall, Ninety-nine bottles of beer. If one of those bottles should happen to fall. . . .

JAKE. (*extremely tense, he screams and steps*) Ninety-eight bottles of beer on the wall. (*quicker*) Ninety-eight bottles of beer on the wall, ninety-eight bottles of beer. If one of those bottles should happen to fall . . .

MICKEY. (*steps*) Ninety-seven bottles of beer on the wall. (*quicker still*) Ninety-seven bottles of beer on the wall, ninety-seven bottles of beer. If one of those bottles should happen to fall. . . .

JAKE. (*He takes three deep breaths and is about to take a step when there is a loud explosion. Screams.*)

MICKEY. Jesus Christmas.

JAKE. Was that human or what? God damn that's some spooky shit.

MICKEY. Sounded like Rogers to me.

JAKE. That didn't sound like shit to me.

MICKEY. It was Rogers.

JAKE. How the hell could you tell?

MICKEY. It was Rogers.

JAKE. Who do you think you are, James Bond?

MICKEY. Believe me it was Rogers.

JAKE. Shit. (*pause*) Sucker owed me a can of peaches. Shit.

MICKEY. Dumb dead fucker. (*both laugh*)

JAKE. Man, sorry-ass Rogers. That sucker musta snapped or some shit. You know what I'm saying. Sucker was out, home, done his tour. He was home six months and working with his old man.

MICKEY. I know.

JAKE. I mean during his first tour all he ever would talk about was going home. How wonderful it was all going to be. How he was going to do this, that, and the other thing. Then he gets out and six months later he's back here up to his ass in shit.

MICKEY. Yeah.

JAKE. It don't make no sense.

MICKEY. What?

JAKE. I don't understand. What the hell happened that made him come back to this fucking jungle paradise?

MICKEY. Don't know.

JAKE. You ever hear him talk about that dream house he was building for his wife when he got out? He spent every frigging minute of every frigging day for about five months planning that house. One day I heard him counting how many nails he was going to need. What kind and how much they cost. Another time we're in the middle of a fucking shelling and he's sitting there deciding on what kind of tile he should use in the bathroom. He had everything worked out right down to the molding around the linen closet.

MICKEY. Yeah.

JAKE. I don't understand it. What happened when he got out? Man, he was home. Did he ever say anything about it to you?

MICKEY. Not to me.

JAKE. He musta been fugazi, right? I mean my ass gets out of here and home, my ass stays out of here and home. He's crazy right?

MICKEY. Maybe.

JAKE. What?

MICKEY. Just what I said, maybe.

JAKE. I know what maybe means, Mickey. I just don't understand it. He never mentioned anything . . .

MICKEY. (*cuts him off*) I said no. So drop it.

JAKE. You know sometimes you really piss me off, you know, Mickey. Why don't you drop your bad-ass-jungle-fighter routine? You be talking like some John Wayne movie.

MICKEY. And you be talking like some ghetto nigger. (*imitates JAKE*) "My man . . . you be talking . . . " Every other word out of your mouth is shit. Why don't you drop *your* gig. Not only are you *not* black, you grew up on frigging Long Island.

JAKE. Right.

MICKEY. Yeah, you're god damn right. (*pause*)

JAKE. Look, Mick, I just wanted to know about Rogers and you keep giving me the slip. You don't have to get so hot. I thought maybe he said something to you.

MICKEY. Well, there's nothing to know.

JAKE. Alright.

MICKEY. Just forget it. I don't want to talk about it.

JAKE. Alright, Jesus. (*pause*) O.K. I'm ready.

MICKEY. Give me a minute. OK, what do you call a two hundred pound mouse?

JAKE. OK what do you call a two hundred pound mouse? (*prepares to take a step*) I'm going. I'm going. Watch me, Mick. I'm going. Here I go. "No-clicks Jakey." Watch me, Mick. I'm incredible.

MICKEY. Easy, Jakey. Come on, baby.

JAKE. OK I'm going. No clicks. I'm going. (*Screams as he steps.*) Whoa, no clicks, right, Mick? How about it? In-fucking-credible or what?

MICKEY. (*laughs*) Right, in-frigging-credible.

JAKE. Right. Hit me. What do you call a two hundred pound mouse?

MICKEY. Sir.

JAKE. Sir? Priceless. One of a kind . . . priceless, I mean just priceless. (*Laughter continues and as it trails off there is a pause.*)

JAKE. Mick?

MICKEY. I know. It's alright, Jakey.

JAKE. Yeah same here. (*pause*)

JAKE. Mick?

MICKEY. Yeah?

JAKE. Ah, I don't know. . . .

MICKEY. Like brothers, Jake, better than brothers. . . .

JAKE. (*smiles*) Yeah. (*awkward pause*)

MICKEY. Two hundred pound mouse called sir. Priceless right?

JAKE. Yeah. (*pause*)

JAKE. Mick, why don't you want to tell me what Rogers told you?

MICKEY. What?

JAKE. I heard you two.

MICKEY. You didn't hear shit.

JAKE. What did Rogers mean when he said he couldn't get home.

MICKEY. Where did you hear that?

JAKE. Late one night I woke up and I heard you and Rogers talking and he was crying and moaning.

MICKEY. I don't remember.

JAKE. Cut the shit, Mick. It was right after he got back here. He went home didn't he?

MICKEY. Yeah, he was running his old man's construction company and building his fucking dream house.

JAKE. Then what did he mean when he said he couldn't get

home? It doesn't make no sense. He went home, he was home. What did he mean? What happened when he got out? Come on, Mick, please, I got to know. I'm out of here in two months.

MICKEY. He said some bullshit about not fitting in. . . . I don't know. . . . and uh . . . that his wife wouldn't let him paint the living room yellow.

JAKE. Shit. She wouldn't let him paint the living room yellow? What kind of twisted moronic bullshit is that? I get out of here and my girl can paint my *ass* yellow if she wants to. That sucker was definitely fried.

MICKEY. I guess.

JAKE. Well what the hell else could it have been?

MICKEY. Looks to me like Rogers wrote himself a starring role in a fucking Disney movie and when he got home the movie wasn't playing. (*pause*)

JAKE. That's some spooky shit.

MICKEY. Right? Hey, what the hell do I know? Maybe Rogers was just a basket case. Maybe the fucker was fugazi.

JAKE. Yeah, right. Talk about fugazi. There was this guy over with the 101st. Whenever somebody in his squad would get zapped, he would go over and stick his hands in the guy's wound. He said he liked the warm feeling, liked feeling the guy's life.

MICKEY. A frigging poet. (*pointing to his crotch*) Tell him to feel this life.

JAKE. I always had a helluva hard time getting to sleep around that guy.

MICKEY. (*laughs*) Right? (*long pause*)

JAKE. Mick, not for nothing, but do you think about home much?

MICKEY. (*just laughs*)

JAKE. I know.

MICKEY. Let it go, Jakey. Out here you dream at your own fucking risk.

JAKE. I know . . . it's just, . . . well, I don't know . . . shit, twelve months of saying to yourself home, home, home, and then

MICKEY. (*cuts him off*) Hey. Come on we gotta keep moving. (*pause*)

MICKEY. OK, I'm ready.

JAKE. Ninety-seven bottles of beer on the wall, (*lights begin to fade*) ninety-seven bottles of beer. If one of those bottles should happen to fall. . . . (*lights out*)

THE END

Cover

by

Jeffrey Sweet

with

Stephen Johnson and Sandra Hastie

COVER by Jeffrey Sweet
with Stephen Johnson and Sandra Hastie

1st Production December 15, 1986

Director. . . . . .Larry Deckel
Sets. . . . . John Saari
Lights. . . . . .John Ebbert
Costumes. . . . . Kim Brown

CAST

MARTY. . . . . PHILIP HINCH
FRANK. . . . . DAVID GARCIA
DIANE. . . . . .AMANDA RAMBO

SETTING

An office.

All programs and publicity materials for this play must carry the
following notice:

FIRST PRODUCED BY ACTORS
THEATRE OF LOUISVILLE

Cover

AT RISE: An office. FRANK is working at his desk. MARTY enters.

MARTY. Work, work, work.

FRANK. Oh, Marty.

MARTY. I'm early.

FRANK. You're early.

MARTY. If I'm interrupting . . .

FRANK. No, this is nothing. Just odds and ends.

MARTY. Nice office.

FRANK. Oh, that's right—you've never been up here, have you?

MARTY. No, this is the first time.

FRANK. Well, you've got to take a look out this window. I've got a view that will knock your eyes out. My big status symbol.

MARTY. You've got to be good, they give you a window like this. They've got to like you.

FRANK. See Jersey over there?

MARTY. I'll be damned, Jersey.

FRANK. What's great is to watch thunderstorms come over the Hudson. Hell of a show. Lightning and huge gothic clouds.

MARTY. Always said that was the best thing that could happen to New Jersey.

FRANK. Well, OK.

MARTY. No, I'm impressed. I really am. This is very nice.

FRANK. Yes, I'm very . . .

MARTY. So, you all set and ready to go?

FRANK. Just let me put this stuff away.

MARTY. Take your time.

FRANK. Where's Diane?

MARTY. Oh, she'll be along in a few minutes. I told her to meet me here. She had an appointment crosstown, so I figured . . .

FRANK. Sure.

MARTY. Actually, I'm glad I got here a little earlier. There's a favor I want to ask of you.

FRANK. Ask away.

MARTY. OK. Well, see, as a topic of conversation, it may come up during the evening where I was last night. And it would make it a lot easier if we could decide between us that I was with you.

FRANK. To say that?

MARTY. Not to say necessarily, but to sort of give the impression that we were together. It would make things a lot simpler for me. I mean, if it comes up.

FRANK. You want me to say . . .

MARTY. Just to say . . .

FRANK. That you and I . . .

MARTY. That we were . . .

FRANK. Together . . .

MARTY. Together . . .

FRANK. Last night.

MARTY. Yeah.

FRANK. You want me to lie.

MARTY. Well . . .

FRANK. Not "well." You want me to lie.

MARTY. Well . . .

FRANK. That's what you're asking.

MARTY. I wouldn't put it . . .

FRANK. Is that what you're asking?

MARTY. Well, yes.

FRANK. To lie?

MARTY. A little bit. Just to give the impression so that Diane won't worry. To avoid confusion and upset for her.

FRANK. I see. You want me to do a favor for you for her.

MARTY. I couldn't have said it better myself.

FRANK. Where were you last night? I mean, I have to know.

MARTY. It doesn't matter.

FRANK. Well, yes, it does. I have to know whether you're wanting me to tell a white lie or a black lie.

MARTY. It's a white lie.

FRANK. How white? I mean, where were you?

MARTY. I was out.

FRANK. Alone? With someone?

MARTY. With someone.

FRANK. Yeah?

MARTY. Diane wouldn't understand.

FRANK. A woman?

MARTY. She'd take it the wrong way.

FRANK. You were out with another woman.

MARTY. Yes, I was out with another woman.

FRANK. I see. And that's a white lie?

MARTY. It's no big deal.

FRANK. I'm sorry, I can't do it.

MARTY. Hey, really, it's no big deal.

FRANK. No, I wouldn't feel good about it.

MARTY. Why not? It's just a little favor.

FRANK. It's not a little . . . You're asking me to lie to her. You don't understand. She's my friend.

MARTY. Aren't I your friend?

FRANK. You're my friend and she's my friend. But she's not my friend because you're my friend. I mean, it's not that you and I have a primary friendship and she's a secondary friend by extension. You're both primary friends.

MARTY. I understand that.

FRANK. You don't break that trust.

MARTY. I'm not asking you to break that trust. I'm asking you to spare her confusion and upset.

FRANK. You're asking me to lie to her.

MARTY. To give a different impression of the truth.

FRANK. A false impression, which is a lie.

MARTY. You've never told a lie in your life?

FRANK. That's not the issue.

MARTY. Of course it's the issue. You're saying you don't tell lies.

FRANK. I'm saying I will not tell *this* lie.

MARTY. How do you decide when you will or will not tell a lie?

FRANK. I try not to lie.

MARTY. But what makes you decide if you'll tell a given lie? Say that an opportunity for a lie presents itself—how do you decide if you'll tell it?

FRANK. This is not the issue.

MARTY. You have told lies, haven't you? You've told lies in the past.

FRANK. I have, but that has nothing to do with this.

MARTY. You just won't tell a lie for me.

FRANK. I don't want to tell an active lie, no.

MARTY. Well, are you going to tell her that I was out with another woman last night?

FRANK. No, of course not.

MARTY. Then isn't that creating a false impression? Isn't that, in fact, a lie?

FRANK. That's a passive lie, my not telling something.

MARTY. Ah, that's different.

FRANK. It is.

MARTY. A difference in kind, right? Active versus passive.

FRANK. There *is* a difference, whether you see it or not.

MARTY. Would you care to elaborate?

FRANK. What do you mean?

MARTY. On the distinction. Active, passive.

FRANK. What does this have to do with . . . ?

MARTY. If we correlate an active lie as being a lie you won't tell and a passive lie as a lie you will, then perhaps we can find that point in the grey area between where we can come to an understanding.

FRANK. Look, I don't want to lie to her.

MARTY. I'm not asking you to *want* to.

FRANK. You're just asking me to do it.

MARTY. Yes, as a favor to a friend.

FRANK. No, I don't want to.

MARTY. You do lots of things you don't want to do. Everybody does.

FRANK. The things that I sometimes do that I don't want to do are things that I have to do. I don't have to do this. I don't have to break that trust.

MARTY. No, and we don't have to be friends, either.

FRANK. Oh, come on. Are you saying if I won't lie for you we won't be friends any more?

MARTY. Of course not. I'm just asking you for a favor.

FRANK. I can't do it.

MARTY. Can't means won't.

FRANK. Can't means can't.

MARTY. Can't means won't.

FRANK. Can't means can't.

MARTY. No, you could.

FRANK. I couldn't.

MARTY. You *could.*

FRANK. I couldn't.

MARTY. Your mouth could say the words. Physically, your mouth could say the words.

FRANK. I couldn't do it.

MARTY. Of course you could.

FRANK. No, I couldn't.

MARTY. You could, but what you're saying is you won't.

FRANK. I'm saying I can't.

MARTY. You're saying you won't.

FRANK. I'm saying . . . OK, I'm saying I won't because I can't.

MARTY. But you *could.*

FRANK. I wouldn't if I could, but I can't so I won't. Anyway, you don't want me to lie for you.

MARTY. Yes, I do.

FRANK. I'm a terrible liar. She'd see right through me.

MARTY. How do you know until you try?

FRANK. Look, I'm not going to tell her where you were. I mean, I couldn't because I don't know.

MARTY. I was at Marvin Gardens. That's on the West Side.

FRANK. I don't want to know. Don't tell me any more.

MARTY. Barbara Schaeffer.

FRANK. I don't want to know who.

MARTY. Barbara Schaeffer.

FRANK. Barbara Schaeffer?

MARTY. See, now you know.

FRANK. I wish you hadn't told me.

MARTY. But you know, and if you don't tell Diane that means you've already lied. Passive-shmassive, it's a lie, and if you've gone that far, why not go a little farther for a friend?

FRANK. Look, you can argue rings around me, but I'm not going to.

MARTY. OK, sorry I asked.

FRANK. I wish you'd understand.

MARTY. It really is a hell of a nice office. You should be very proud. (*A beat. DIANE Enters.*)

DIANE. I've found you at last.

FRANK. You have trouble?

DIANE. You could've at least left a trail of breadcrumbs. So, you guys ready to go?

FRANK. In a second.

DIANE. Hey, nice view.

FRANK. You like it?

DIANE. That's Jersey, isn't it?

MARTY. You can see thunderstorms, Frank says.

DIANE. Oh really? That must be exciting.

FRANK. What, I don't get a kiss?

DIANE. Absolutely! (*She kisses Frank.*)

FRANK. Hey, you look swell.

DIANE. In contrast to . . . ?

FRANK. No, of course not.

DIANE. Thank you.

FRANK. That's a nice outfit.

DIANE. I'm glad you like it.

FRANK. It really is. I really do. (*FRANK goes offstage with a file.*)

DIANE. (*To MARTY:*) So, how was your day?

MARTY. Fine.

DIANE. You and Jacobs get that thing cleared up?

MARTY. No big problem.

DIANE. I thought you were worried.

MARTY. Not seriously. We sat down, we talked.

DIANE. You compromised.

MARTY. I didn't have to.

DIANE. It must be a relief.

MARTY. And your interview?

DIANE. Nothing definite.

MARTY. But there's interest?

DIANE. They didn't say no.

MARTY. That's half the battle.

DIANE. Yeah.

MARTY. Fingers crossed. (*FRANK returns.*)

DIANE. You got here early, hunh?

MARTY. Just a few minutes ago.

DIANE. You've got a lot of papers on your desk, Frank. You must work awfully hard.

FRANK. It just looks that way. Gives the impression I'm earning my money, which, of course, I'm not.

DIANE. Oh, no, I know you. Industrious. Kind, loyal, honest, brave. You're the only person I know who lives up to . . . what is it?

MARTY. (*a little dig*) The Boy Scout code.

DIANE. (*an immediate echo*) The Boy Scout code.

FRANK. I wouldn't know. I wasn't a Scout.

DIANE. I can see you loaded down with merit badges.

FRANK. Yes, well now, *Touch of Evil* starts at 7:10 at the museum, so that means we should figure out what restaurant in the area . . .

MARTY. We should be pushing along, right.

FRANK. There's not a big hurry, but if we want to have a few drinks first . . .

DIANE. (*To MARTY:*) Hey . . .

MARTY. How are ya?

DIANE. What are you doing?

MARTY. Just saying hi to you. (*a beat*)

DIANE. We have to be at the museum at what?

FRANK. Well, by seven at least.

DIANE. So, where shall we eat?

FRANK. How does Italian sound, or are you on a diet and don't want that, or what? Chinese?

DIANE. Do you think I should be on a diet?

FRANK. Women always seem to be on diets. Men, too. People in general.

DIANE. Women aren't always on diets. Some women diet. The heavy variety. They tend to diet.

FRANK. I can remember you being on some pretty screwy diets.

DIANE. You think I'm screwy?

FRANK. No, of course not. I didn't say that.

DIANE. I'm sorry. I'm a little weird tonight. The ozone or something.

FRANK. Sure, I mean, air quality does . . .

DIANE. (*Interrupting; to MARTY:*) You didn't get home till really late last night.

MARTY. I know.

DIANE. I wasn't even awake when you got home.

MARTY. I know. I didn't want to disturb you.

DIANE. Listen to the man! My favorite thing in the world is to wrap my arms around him in bed and he says he doesn't want to disturb me. And you got up and left early this morning, too.

MARTY. I know. I had to get out.

DIANE. Away from me?

MARTY. No, no, of course not. I just had to leave.

DIANE. Why?

MARTY. I had someplace to be.

DIANE. Oh.

MARTY. Preparing for the Jacobs thing, you know.

DIANE. Yeah.

FRANK. Do you want me to leave? Would you rather be alone or . . . ?

DIANE. (*interrupting*) I promised myself I wasn't going to ask this question. I mean, I was in the bathroom and I combed my hair and I looked in the mirror and I said to myself, "You're looking good, Diane. You're looking very good."

FRANK. You look terrific.

DIANE. (*quiet, intense*) Where were you last night? Where were you till so late?

MARTY. (*a beat, then —*) I was with Frank all night long. Isn't that right, Frank? (*a beat*)

FRANK. Yeah, that's right. He was. With me. We were . . .

DIANE. With Frank?

MARTY. Yes. Is that what you were so worried about?

DIANE. Yes, I'm sorry. It's stupid.

FRANK. We were playing . . .

MARTY. Playing . . .

FRANK. Poker.

MARTY. Cards. I didn't want to tell you because, well, I know you don't like me gambling.

DIANE. No.

MARTY. And I lost a little last night.

FRANK. Yeah, I zapped him for a little.

DIANE. How much?

FRANK. Forty-something. He made me promise not to tell.

DIANE. I see. Well . . .

FRANK. Tell you what, dinner's on me tonight, OK?

DIANE. (*She knows they've been lying now. She looks at FRANK very directly and says—*) Why not? (*a beat*)

MARTY. I guess we'd better get going, hunh?

(*DIANE nods. She exits first. FRANK and MARTY exchange a look before Exiting. Lights fade out.*)

The Duck Pond

by
Ara Watson

THE DUCK POND by Ara Watson

1st Production December 18, 1981

Director. . . . . Robert Spera
Sets. . . . . Jonathan W. Sprouse
Lights. . . . . Pip Gordon

CAST

RACHEL. . . . . HELEN PETTIT
JOHN. . . . . NEIL LARSON
ELIZABETH. . . . . PAMELA KORNHAAS

SETTING

A pond in a park.

TIME

Early afternoon of a spring day.

All programs and publicity materials for this play must carry the following notice:

COMMISSIONED AND FIRST PRODUCED BY ACTORS THEATRE OF LOUISVILLE

The Duck Pond

SCENE: *The bank of a pond that flows through the campus of a mid-America university. There is a park bench facing the pond (the audience) with a trash container by it.*

AT RISE: *RACHEL, about twenty years old and twenty pounds overweight, is standing on the bank throwing bread to the ducks in the pond from a paper sack she's holding. Her books and another paper sack are on the bench behind her.*

RACHEL. OK, here goes. (*She throws a piece of bread.*) Oh, come on. You can do better than that. You have to at least try. If I'm going to try, you have to try. One more time — and watch out for old Marmaduke there. OK. One — two — Oh, on the count of three. OK? OK. One — two — three (*She throws. Excited.*) No, no, to your left! To your — ! Wha — ? I don't believe it. How could you miss that one? Well, don't look at me. I threw it practically right to you. (*She eats a few bread pieces.*) Nope. No more special favors. You'll have to take your chances with the rest. (*throws a handful*) Bet you'll miss me next week, won't you? (*ELIZABETH and JOHN Enter. They are a year or two older than RACHEL, very "clean cut," dressed neatly — ELIZABETH in dress, low heels. They are carrying books.*) Well, I'll only be gone for a week. You won't —

ELIZABETH. (*interrupting*) Rachel?

RACHEL. (*Startled, she turns quickly, dropping her sack.*) What?

JOHN. (*smiling*) We've been looking for you, Rachel.

ELIZABETH. (*smiling*) We surely didn't mean to frighten you.

RACHEL. No . . . no. I was . . .

JOHN. You dropped your sack. (*Putting his books on the bench, he picks up the sack and the crumbs which have fallen out.*) Here. We better pick this up for you.

RACHEL. I can. (*But she doesn't.*)

ELIZABETH. (*coming to her*) It's a beautiful day, isn't it? I would say spring is definitely here. (*kisses her on the cheek*) I can certainly understand why you sneaked out of your study cubicle.

RACHEL. I didn't.

JOHN. (*Gently reprimanding her with a smile.*) Hey . . . Rachel.

RACHEL. I mean . . . I just took a little break, is all . . .

215

JOHN. (*rising*) You know what the regs say, though.

ELIZABETH. (*pointing*) Oh, would you look at that? (*laughs*) Aren't they wonderfully funny when they take off from the water? There are so many different kinds. Do you know much about them, Rachel?

RACHEL. I know . . . a little. I've . . . been studying them.

ELIZABETH. (*looking all around her*) I can never quite get over what a beautiful campus we have. So much space. We're very, very lucky.

JOHN. I think the word is fortunate, Elizabeth.

ELIZABETH. (*smiles*) Of course. (*To RACHEL:*) And I, for one, am most grateful to be here.

RACHEL. Yes.

ELIZABETH. "Yes?"

RACHEL. I'm grateful, too.

ELIZABETH. See, John. I told you.

JOHN. Yeah. Yeah, I'm real glad to hear that. Good. Good.

ELIZABETH. (*To RACHEL:*) Are you planning to go home for spring break next week?

RACHEL. (*smiling*) Yes. I haven't seen my folks since the fall.

ELIZABETH. Now, won't that be nice? See, I'm grateful, John —and I'm sure Rachel is, too—that we can live and work and learn here with God-fearing and God-loving people, with our family in Jesus.

JOHN. Praise the Lord.

ELIZABETH. Praise the Lord.

RACHEL. Praise the Lord.

ELIZABETH. We're given so much here and so little is asked of us in return.

JOHN. (*To RACHEL:*) I've forgotten whether you went to State or University last year.

RACHEL. (*quietly*) State.

ELIZABETH. Now, John, don't bring all that up. That's past history. Rachel doesn't need to be reminded of how unhappy she was before she came here—how she didn't have any friends. Do you, Rachel? (*RACHEL shakes her head.*) No, of course not.

RACHEL. I'm very happy here, Elizabeth.

ELIZABETH. That's wonderful to hear you say. (*She embraces Rachel.*) I love you, Rachel. You're like a sister to me. You are a sister to me in the Lord.

RACHEL. I'm sorry, Elizabeth. I . . . I won't break regs anymore.

ELIZABETH. Pray about it.

RACHEL. I will. Thank you. I'll go back in now.

(*RACHEL picks up her things from the bench as JOHN and ELIZABETH watch her. As she starts off, ELIZABETH nods slightly to JOHN.*)

JOHN. Rachel. (*RACHEL stops.*) We haven't finished our business with you.

RACHEL. But I promise —

JOHN. The Council sent us to talk to you and I'm afraid it's more serious than your bad study habits.

ELIZABETH. Would you like to sit down?

RACHEL. No.

JOHN. Sit down, Rachel. (*She does so.*) I think you ought to know that Elizabeth and I went way out on a limb for you today.

RACHEL. Why? How? What — ?

ELIZABETH. You must let him finish.

JOHN. We didn't want to see you just kicked out.

RACHEL. Kicked out?!

ELIZABETH. Shhhh.

JOHN. I don't know how you can sit there and act surprised. Did you think they were just going to forget about it? I'm telling you, it was very hard for Elizabeth and me to stand up in front of the other members of the Council and ask for a chance to come talk to you before final decision. It took a lot of courage on our part, Rachel — a lot of courage.

ELIZABETH. Everyone else was saying, "We've already given her a second chance — it didn't do any good. What good would another chance do?" But we said we were just sure there must be an explanation, a reason . . . That you were too precious to be —

JOHN. (*interrupting*) Stand up, Rachel. Go on. (*She does.*) When you came to us at the first of the year, we — the school, the Council — accepted you on one condition. Do you remember that condition? Well? Do you? (*RACHEL stands with lowered head.*) Stand up! You know what I see when I look at you now? I sure don't see a Christian girl. I see a fat girl. I see a fat girl who has broken her word to all those who have loved and trusted her.

RACHEL. I didn't!

JOHN. What do you mean you didn't? How can you say that — "you didn't?" I was there, both of us were, when you signed that oath that by the end of this year you would be regulation weight. And, when you weren't losing any by the end of last semester and we talked to you and you said you were trying, but it was slow, you were changing your eating habits, you'd be down by the middle of the next semester, et cetera, et cetera, we believed you. We trusted you. Were you lying from the beginning? Were you just sitting back laughing at all our help, all our concern for you?

RACHEL. I've tried! I have tried! It's my metabolism.

JOHN. Meta—! You see, Elizabeth. She's going to go right on deceiving. (*He picks up the second paper sack and dumps out two candy bars and a cupcake.*) The body is the temple of the Lord and if you don't care about your body, then you don't care about the Lord. Come on, Elizabeth. We're going to have to go face the Council with this.

ELIZABETH. I'm very hurt, Rachel.

RACHEL. I wasn't going to eat it.

JOHN. Were you going to feed it to the ducks? (*toward her*) You know what the Council will decide after they get our report?

ELIZABETH. You will be asked to leave, Rachel.

JOHN. You'll be told to leave.

RACHEL. No, I don't want to go. I can't . . .

JOHN. You won't have any choice. God needs a strong army. We don't have any room for liars and weaklings.

ELIZABETH. You'll never be able to come back. We will never speak your name again. We will erase you from our minds and our hearts.

RACHEL. Oh, don't. Please, please. I can. I know I can. I promise. I promise, I promise, I promise!

JOHN. You promised before.

RACHEL. And I tried! Nobody ever believes me! I tried!

JOHN. You see? You're still lying!

RACHEL. No, I'm—

ELIZABETH. John, maybe—

JOHN. Not while she's still lying! We won't accept another promise born in a lie!

ELIZABETH. (*gently*) Rachel, admit you lied and ask for forgiveness.

JOHN. She doesn't want to be forgiven.

RACHEL. I do!

ELIZABETH. Then ask before it's too late. Now. Ask now.

RACHEL. I do ask.

ELIZABETH. You must say the words.

Rachel. (*quietly*) Forgive me.

John. What? I can't hear you.

Elizabeth. Louder, Rachel.

Rachel. I did.

Elizabeth. Louder, Rachel.

Rachel. (*a little louder*) Forgive me.

John. For what, Rachel? "Forgive me" for what?

Rachel. (*the crying begins*) For . . . you know . . . for lying.

John. And for what else?

Rachel. (*confused*) For . . . for . . . I don't . . .

John. Don't you want to be forgiven for being fat? For letting the Devil have control of your mind and your body? You're fat, aren't you? Aren't you?! (*RACHEL nods.*) You've got a fat, ugly body! Say it!

Rachel. (*mumbling*) I'm . . . fat.

Elizabeth. Louder, Rachel. Cast Satan out with the truth.

Rachel. I'm fat.

John. Again.

Rachel. (*louder*) I'm fat.

Elizabeth. Again!

Rachel. (*louder*) I'm fat! I'm fat! (*louder*) I'm fat! (*almost yelling*) I'm fat and I'm fat and I'm fat!

Elizabeth. (*under*) Praise God!

Rachel. And I'm fat and I'm ugly! I'm ugly! I'm—

(*RACHEL breaks down sobbing. JOHN and ELIZABETH stand and look at her a moment, then smile at each other. ELIZABETH slowly moves in and enfolds her.*)

Elizabeth. Praise the Lord. There, there. You've faced it. You have stood up to it. It's all right now. Just feel the cleansing power of the Lord. (*She smiles at JOHN.*) We love you, Rachel. God loves you. We'll talk to the Council and see what we can do. You can stay here at school during the spring break. You won't have to go home. We'll help you. We'll be with you and pray with you. (*ELIZABETH nods to JOHN, who comes over and puts his arm around RACHEL and begins leading her off.*) Go with John, now. Go with John to the Prayer Temple.

John. (*Exiting, he quietly talks to RACHEL, who is still crying and is now clinging to JOHN.*) Jesus will help you. You know that. You've seen it over and over again. He loves you and he wants to keep you with his chosen, but you must learn that a good soldier is an obedient soldier, and the Lord needs good, healthy soldiers . . . (*off*)

(*During JOHN and RACHEL's Exit, ELIZABETH has been gathering the things on the bench. She finds there are still crumbs in the sack, so she walks closer to the pond and throws them in. She watches as the ducks gobble them up and she smiles warmly at them.*)

ELIZABETH. You don't care, do you? You big old fat lazy things. (*And, with a smile, she turns and Exits.*)

LIGHTS

THE END

Looking Good

by
John W. Williams

LOOKING GOOD by John Walker Williams

1st Production May 28, 1985

Director. . . . . Robert Spera
Sets. . . . . .Paul Owen
Lights. . . . . Janine Silver
Costumes. . . . . Wendy Juren

CAST

MITCHELL. . . . . DINK O'NEAL
STUART. . . . . DOUG WERT
HOUSTON (V.O.). . . . . CRAIG JOHNSON

SETTING

A space shuttle cockpit.

CHARACTERS

MITCHELL
STUART
HOUSTON (Voice Off)

Looking Good

SCENE: Darkness. Voices over a radio.

MITCHELL. I've never seen the "northern six" so clear. They don't twinkle up here. Sirius and the twins Castor and Pollux are the brightest. What a beautiful sight. We can clearly see the western coast of Africa and the Canary Islands . . . What do you see out your window, Stuart? Stuart? (*sigh*) Looks like I can see Spain and Portugal. We've pitched down a bit to get a better view.

HOUSTON. (*Capcom*) That's fine, Columbia. We'd like you to position the antenna at pitch three-zero, yaw two-seven-zero, go to react.

MITCHELL. Roger, we copy.

(*AT RISE: Lights up on two astronauts sitting in the cockpit of their space shuttle: MITCHELL, in the Commander's chair on his left, and STUART in the pilot's chair on his right. They are surrounded by consoles — displays, switches, buttons — which keep them pretty busy. Most of the equipment, however, is imagined and mimed. They wear headgear and headsets with attached mikes. Their uniforms resemble tailored jumpsuits with patches and special attachments. There are periodic sounds of transmission static, beeps & chirps, etc. They speak with experience.*)

HOUSTON. Looking good, Columbia.

MITCHELL. Altitude six hundred thirty-nine thousand feet, registering apogee one hundred thirty-two nautical miles, perigee fifty-seven nautical miles.

(*MITCHELL glances at STUART, who is sitting immobile, staring out his window.*)

HOUSTON. Roger, Columbia. In space, not yet in orbit. Coming up on ten minutes to High Orbit Insertion Burn. Velocity eighteen thousand feet per second, approximately thirty-one hundred nautical miles downrange.

MITCHELL. *Mark*, ten minutes to High Orbit Insertion Burn. (*pulling mike away from his mouth, whispering hoarsely*) Lighten up, Stuart. (*Back to Houston:*) All conditions go.

HOUSTON. Sixteen minutes, mission elapsed time.

STUART. (*With hand over mike.*) Look, it doesn't make any sense! What are they doing down there?

MITCHELL. (*Surprised.*) Take it easy, Stuart. I'm sure they're working on the problem.

STUART. What do you mean, take it easy? We don't even know what happened. It's your neck too, y'know.

MITCHELL. Why wasn't it traced immediately? What buttons did you push to initiate the roll?

STUART. Starboard and port thrusters, right here. (*Mitchell leans over cautiously.*)

MITCHELL. What's that button over there?

STUART. Where?

MITCHELL. On this end.

STUART. Here?

MITCHELL. Yeah. Read it to me.

STUART. "Roll sequence engage clearance."

MITCHELL. Read the one next to it.

STUART. "Bay Pod Eject Number One." (*Stuart does a double-take.*)

STUART. Wait a minute. How come your side doesn't have that? See what I mean? I *told* them it wasn't safe. I recommended, I *strongly* recommended they change the console design. I *knew* it would be a problem. Did they listen?

MITCHELL. Stuart, there's no reason to—

STUART. How do I explain to Houston that I accidently hit the wrong button and activated pod number one? (*In a voice.*) "Ah, Houston, we got a runaway experiment." "Right, don't worry about it boys, these things happen."

MITCHELL. Really, Stuart. Houston will understand.

STUART. Oh, will they?

MITCHELL. (*Pause.*) Well . . .

STUART. That's what I'm afraid of. (*Pause. Into his mike.*) Houston, when will you have that state vector?

HOUSTON. Stand by. (*Beat.*) That will be some time yet, Columbia.

STUART. Why don't they have that data yet? Are they purposely dragging their feet?

MITCHELL. Stuart, relax. They have a lot to do.

STUART. Relax! I'm the one who lost the payload pod and I'm the one who'll get canned. No reprimand, no official decision, just a debriefing. And that'll be the end.

MITCHELL. Aw, c'mon Stuart. You know it's not like that anymore.

STUART. Oh yeah? What about Davis? Forgot to stow the toilet before turnaround. When they inverted for re-entry . . . hundreds of pretty little yellow globules floating around the cabin. He's doing P.R. in Houston, now. (*Beat.*) We got to figure out how to save that stupid experiment.

MITCHELL. I think it's more important that we get this shuttle into orbit first, *then* worry about it.

STUART. But why hasn't Houston called us on this? (*Suspiciously.*) They're waiting for *us* to say something first . . .

MITCHELL. (*With authority.*) Houston doesn't know. They're not monitoring those functions.

STUART. You're kidding.

MITCHELL. No payload telemetry will be transmitted until we begin orbital deployment operations. You know that. Concentrate on flying.

STUART. After all, it's just another Bell Labs experiment.

MITCHELL. (*Sarcastically.*) Right. Just another four-million-dollar gravity-less experiment.

HOUSTON. Columbia, Houston. Our position checks show you to be a little long downrange.

MITCHELL. Roger, Houston, stand by. (*Scans his board, punches a button.*) AGS showing rate two feet per second above pre-set optimum. Altitude rate is zero-point-one. Shall we revise?

(*Stuart picks up a manual with indexed tabs and begins leafing through it with slight desperation.*)

HOUSTON. Negative, Columbia. Latest estimate for Extra-Vehicular Activity is fifty-eight-o-three, top of the orbit, copy?

MITCHELL. Roger, Houston, fifty-eight-o-three.

HOUSTON. Coming up on seven minutes to High Orbit Insertion Burn. Columbia, our systems engineer tells us the top of your bird is getting pretty hot, suggest you roll for a minute and let the sun warm your belly, over.

MITCHELL. Roger, Houston, initiating short PTC, over. (*He punches several buttons. Beat. To Stuart:*) What're you looking for?

STUART. A way to reset this circuit break.

MITCHELL. Look. I'll put the computer through a standard on-board systems check. Why don't you run a check of the payload sensors, bay connections, and environment security?

STUART. All right. (*They proceed to flip switches, punch their keyboard, and watch the displays.*) Mitch, ah . . . I want you to know I'll bear full responsibility for the problem. Like a professional.

MITCHELL. Uh-huh.

STUART. It's a matter of integrity and accountability.

MITCHELL. Right.

STUART. I guess I'm just a little on edge . . .

MITCHELL. (*absently*) That's all right . . .

STUART. I think it's the liquid meat . . . too much gas in those bags.

MITCHELL. Propulsion system and avionics okay.

STUART. All seals are airtight, no breach in any through-hull fittings. The bay seems tight.

MITCHELL. Everything checks out. (*beat*) Funny . . .

STUART. What?

MITCHELL. (*punching keyboard again*) Just a minute.

STUART. What is it?

MITCHELL. It keeps getting hung up on Systems Two . . . there's a problem with the primary fuel cells.

STUART. (*slightly alarmed*) The tanks or the fuel relay?

MITCHELL. (*punches more buttons*) If we have fuel pressure . . .

STUART. Wait, I'm getting a low reading from Main Bus B.

MITCHELL. Then there's no problem with the fuel cells.

STUART. It's just a glitch, it'll clear itself up.

HOUSTON. Columbia, Houston.

STUART. Oh, no.

MITCHELL. Shhh. (*flips switch*) This is Columbia.

HOUSTON. Five minutes to Insertion Burn. Columbia, we're picking up unusual biomed on you. The flight surgeon says your B.P. and heart rate have been uneven over the past ten minutes. Anything wrong, or is it just opening night jitters, over?

STUART. (*quickly*) That's it, Houston. It's breathtaking up here.

HOUSTON. Roger. Columbia, our console shows your on-board computer has had a hardware restart. We're trying to trace the source of this event. Any information, over?

MITCHELL. Yes, we're familiar with the event, believe it was just a glitch. We've performed a routine systems check and it got hung up on the power system, then righted itself. We think it's probably in our console. Nothing serious, but we'll rerun it.

HOUSTON. Columbia, could the problem be on line? Any other counter-indications from your console?

STUART. Possible, but the inboard processor is handling data just fine. (*beat*) We'll take care of it, Houston.

HOUSTON. Roger, Columbia. We'll continue to run tests from here.

STUART. I don't like it. You think Houston knows more than they're letting on?

MITCHELL. We'll run more tests. But first . . . (*He flips a few switches.*) There.

STUART. What will that tell us?

MITCHELL. Everything checks out. (*pointing to various gauges*) Tanks are full, life support systems fully operational, telemetry and guidance systems fine, and (*as he hits a button*) the Main Propulsion system, *there.* (*looks more closely at the display instrument, taps it with his finger.*) What—?!

STUART. Cycle the switch. (*MITCHELL flips the switch back and forth several times. They both watch as it becomes lifeless. They turn and look at each other.*) Oh-oh.

HOUSTON. Columbia, this is Houston.

STUART. (*in mock disbelief*) No! . . .

HOUSTON. In preparation for G-shift and pitch maneuver during burn we'd like you to resume omnifunctional telemetry relay, over.

STUART. No! They'll find it for sure.

MITCHELL. Stuart—we can't tell them no.

STUART. Give me a chance to neutralize the problem first.

MITCHELL. What're you going to do?

HOUSTON. Columbia, do you read?

MITCHELL. Roger, Houston. Ah, we're presently using that computer as a redundant program to check on the recent event in our computer survey . . . A second opinion, Houston.

HOUSTON. (*pause*) Roger, Columbia.

STUART. Quick thinking.

MITCHELL. They didn't sound too thrilled by that one. (*STUART starts to unbuckle himself.*)

STUART. I think I'll have a closer look at the problem.

MITCHELL. Where're you going?

STUART. Back aft to have a closer look.

MITCHELL. Are you crazy? There's no time.

HOUSTON. Three minutes to Insertion Burn.

MITCHELL. If you leave the flight deck Houston will know something's wrong.

STUART. Yeah, well, something *is* wrong.

MITCHELL. Wait 'til after the burn and we begin orbital operations.

HOUSTON. Prepare for automatic release of External Tank.

STUART. (*has an idea, punches buttons*) I've got a better idea.

MITCHELL. What?

STUART. I'll just jettison the messed-up experiment when I release the empty External Fuel Tank.

MITCHELL. (*amazed*) Oh yeah? And how will we explain a missing pod?

STUART. We might not have to. A procedural contingency, circuit break . . . We've got a computer malfunction, loose capture locks, any number of—

MITCHELL. Houston will trace it in a minute. Stuart, really . . . (*beat*) What was that?

STUART. What?

HOUSTON. External Tank separation complete.

MITCHELL. You didn't feel it?

STUART. (*innocently*) What did it feel like, Mitch?

MITCHELL. A . . . shudder. You didn't feel anything?

STUART. So, ah, you don't like my idea?

MITCHELL. Jettisoning the pod? No. I don't,

STUART. (*beat*) That's too bad.

MITCHELL. Why?

STUART. Because I just jettisoned the problem.

MITCHELL. What??

STUART. With the empty tank.

MITCHELL. That was the bang I felt?

STUART. 'Fraid so.

MITCHELL. Stuart—how are we going to explain this?

STUART. We may not have to.

MITCHELL. What are you saying?

STUART. Wait for Houston to find it, then we'll troubleshoot.

HOUSTON. Two minutes to High Orbit Insertion Burn.

MITCHELL. Stuart—(*reconsidering*) Not much time. Okay, I'm about to resume telemetry relay. But first I'm going to change transmitter mode and make some double-checks. (*MITCHELL flips some switches and punches his keyboard. STUART similarly.*) Hey, look at this. The bay is secure, it says all pods are accounted for.

STUART. What? How—?

MITCHELL. But the glitch is back. The computer won't run past this point in the cycle.

STUART. It's hung up on the Main Propulsion System again.

HOUSTON. One minute twenty seconds to burn. Columbia, you may leave the barbecue mode, and please resume complete telemetry relay. (*As MITCHELL is about to respond, STUART cuts him off.*)

STUART. Wait.

MITCHELL. We've got to —

STUART. Tell them we're clearing a program.

HOUSTON. Columbia, we're getting a lot of static, say again please.

MITCHELL. Houston, read you loud and clear. Resuming complete telemetry relay through aft OMNI, low-bit rate. *Mark,* one minute to High Burn.

HOUSTON. Roger, Columbia, we read you. Did you find the source of that event, over?

MITCHELL. (*considering*) Ah, Houston, we believe it was in the program procedure, here in our console. We fed the data through another vent. Exiting solar roll program now.

HOUSTON. Columbia, we're reading a fault in your primary fuel connection — can you confirm, over?

STUART. (*pause; quickly*) Ah, negative. (*nice try*) Do you want to check our target delta-V?

HOUSTON. Columbia, we seem to have a loss-of-contact with your primary fuel monitor. Please advise immediately, over. (*STUART reaches over and hits the telemetry relay, effectively cutting off that problem for Houston.*)

MITCHELL. Are you crazy?

STUART. Ah, Houston, no problem up here, perhaps the problem is in your computers or in the telemetry angulation, over.

HOUSTON. You have no hardware restart and read full thrust capability, over?

STUART. Affirmative, all systems in order. Set for ignition in forty seconds. (*beat*)

HOUSTON. Roger. Prepare for arming.

MITCHELL. Did you take care of the problem in the main propulsion readout?

STUART. It's all set . . . I think.

MITCHELL. You *think*?

STUART. Well, one light says the system is fine, the other says . . .

MITCHELL. Yes?

STUART. It says it isn't there.

MITCHELL. What do you mean, "not there?"

STUART. No vital feedback from it of any kind. It doesn't exist.

HOUSTON. Thirty seconds to burn, you may arm your pyros.

MITCHELL. Thank you, Houston. Initiate arming sequence. *Mark,* logic one. *Mark*, logic two. (*To STUART:*) Let me see that data.

HOUSTON. Columbia, we need the SEC arm circuit breakers closed.

MITCHELL. Will do, Houston. Going in, SEC arm Battery A. Battery B. (*punches his keyboard*) Oh my God.

STUART. See what I mean?

MITCHELL. No, not that—

HOUSTON. Twenty seconds to Burn. SPS Guidance and Navigation three-six-six-three-niner, NOUN forty-eight minus seventy-two plus o-five-one. Okay, boys.

MITCHELL. I don't think that was Bell Labs you jettisoned in such a hurry.

STUART. What? Then what was it?

MITCHELL. When you released our External Tank . . .

HOUSTON. Ten seconds. Horizon check at entry attitude two-niner-eight degrees. Primary ignition check.

STUART. Yes??

MITCHELL. You programmed the emergency fuel dump—

STUART. No. (*chuckle*) I couldn't have. Not our—

MITCHELL. (*hitting a bank of buttons*) Primary ignition *set*.

HOUSTON. Five . . . four . . .

MITCHELL. (*Looking at Stuart*) Three . . .two . . .

STUART. One . . .

(*There is a distinct "click." They do not move. They turn slowly and look at each other. Fade slowly to black as:*)

HOUSTON. Ignition at 26 minutes, target delta-V is now one-o-two-three-forty. How's it look, boys? (*beat*) Columbia, do you copy, over?

BLACKOUT

THE END

Cold Water

A play in ten minutes

by

Lee Blessing

COLD WATER by Lee Blessing

1st Production May 27, 1986

Director. . . . . .Mark Sawyer-Dailey
Sets. . . . . John Saari
Lights. . . . . .Hunt Lewis
Costumes. . . . . Hollis Jenkins-Evans

CAST

AUGUST. . . . . MARK NASH
RUSSELL. . . . . .EDWARD PATRICK CORBETT
JUNE. . . . . HELEN GREENBERG
ERIC. . . . . JEFFREY CROCKETT

CHARACTERS

AUGUST . . . . .mid-twenties graduate teaching assistant
at a major university
RUSSELL. . . . . early twenties. An upperclassman
JUNE. . . . . late teens. A friend of Russell
ERIC. . . . . early twenties. A graduating senior

TIME

Soon.

PLACE

A university.

All programs and publicity material for this play must carry the following notice:

COMMISSIONED AND FIRST PRODUCED BY ACTORS THEATRE OF LOUISVILLE

Cold Water

SCENE: A room.
AT RISE: Lights rise in a single tight spot on AUGUST, who sits on a low, bare stool.)

AUGUST. Last semester I was teaching a seminar in 18th-Century English poetry. Assistant teaching. My section met twice a week. I helped the undergrads with stuff they were having trouble on. It was a pretty loose section. A few of the kids wanted to bring their dogs to class. I said ok. We sat around a long conference table, and the dogs slept under it — they weren't any problem. As time went on, through Swift and Gray and Samuel Johnson, there was really no difficulty at all. I'd discuss the Neo-Classical sensibility, the dogs would sleep, and the kids seemed to listen better if they had something they could pet once in awhile. Then one day I was discussing Alexander Pope's *Essay On Criticism.* It was raining outside, so there were all these wet dogs under the table, and their smell made them a little harder to forget than usual. Still, I was doing pretty well — making Pope as scintillating as he can be for people who've witnessed 20,000 violent deaths on the tube by the time they're 13. I had my kids in a pretty appreciative state of mind, I thought — to the point where they were genuinely admiring the antiquated eloquence of the heroic couplet. They were even compelled, I thought, by Pope's use of juxtaposition to create an unassailable rhetorical advantage. They were honestly impressed by his transformation of name-calling into a high art form. I even imagined that the students who were petting dogs under the table as I spoke were doing so just a little bit faster, just a hint more passionately, as they began to feel for the first time Alexander Pope's own great passion. For the first time, I told myself, these students — even those wearing headphones — can feel Pope's outrage at the slothful, modish, self-aggrandizement of his enemies. For perhaps the one and only time, they can share in Pope's transcendant poetic achievement: the marriage of pure thought to pure expression. They can see his mastery of the couplet for what it really is: the deepest passion of the intellect — fully realized, utterly fulfilled, made manifest and eternally beautiful. Then the dogs started to copulate. Well, not all the dogs; two of the dogs — enough to break the mood. The male was too big for the female, so she started screaming like

233

horses do when they're shot. That sound froze me. The students looked at me for what to do next, but I just sat there—I couldn't move. I couldn't even lift my hands off the table. The dogs were locked together, and when two students finally had the presence of mind to carry them out, they had to carry them out still connected, still screaming, all the way down the hall to the men's room—where, I was informed, cold water was applied. After that, it was hard to use the word couplet. And dogs stayed outside. I saw them out there for days afterward, through the classroom window: smelling each other, mounting and remounting. My students called it pure thought married to pure expression.

(*Lights fade up quickly on the rest of the stage, which is filled with boxes of books. RUSSELL crosses behind AUGUST, carrying more books. His energy is nervous, dark. AUGUST wears a light spring jacket and cords. RUSSELL has on black jeans, boots and a work shirt.*)

RUSSELL. You say something?
AUGUST. No. (*RUSSELL tosses the books in a box.*)
RUSSELL. Gonna burn these books.
AUGUST. Ok.
RUSSELL. They're your books. (*A beat. AUGUST makes no response.*) I could take 'em down to the used bookstore. Sell 'em back. That'd just start the whole thing over, though. Buy 'em, read 'em, sell 'em, Someone else buys 'em, reads 'em . . . knowledge could go on forever like that. (*RUSSELL has gone back for more books and returned, throwing them into the boxes. He's back by the time the preceding speech ends.*) You've been a good roommate.
AUGUST. Thanks.
RUSSELL. For a faggot.
AUGUST. I appreciate it.
RUSSELL. Most fags hate being called fags. But you're real good about it. I think that's smart. You learn a lot more about people if you don't let 'em offend you.

(*JUNE enters. She's dressed in white jeans, white tennis shoes, white t-shirt.*)

JUNE. I got everything in the car.
RUSSELL. Good. August?

AUGUST. What?

RUSSELL. Everything that's in the car—I'm gonna burn it. Ok?

AUGUST. Ok.

RUSSELL. Sure.

AUGUST. Yeah.

RUSSELL. Gonna burn the car, too.

AUGUST. All right.

RUSSELL. It's your car.

AUGUST. Won't need it.

JUNE. When my Dad went in the Army, he drove his car off a bridge. He jumped out just in time. Watched a perfectly good Pontiac fly into the river. (*A beat. RUSSELL turns to her slowly.*)

RUSSELL. So what?

JUNE. I don't know. He just did it.

RUSSELL. I'm talking about *burning* a car, not drowning it.

JUNE. I know.

RUSSELL. Using *fire*. (*a beat*) What in hell are you doing in college?

JUNE. I don't know. (*RUSSELL picks up a box of books, Exits.*) August? You sure you're not going to miss any of these things?

AUGUST. Nope.

(*ERIC Enters. He is clean-cut, in bright, colorful clean clothes. Very cheerful*)

ERIC. Upstairs is all cleaned out.

AUGUST. Completely?

ERIC. Yup. Nothing up there.

AUGUST. Mattresses? Bed frames?

ERIC. All gone.

AUGUST. Rugs?

ERIC. Out the window.

AUGUST. Hangers?

ERIC. Coat hangers, you mean? Out the window. We even untwisted 'em. Threw 'em down like little spears.

AUGUST. Nothing's left.

ERIC. Nope. (*RUSSELL enters and picks up another box. He takes it out.*) Empty walls, empty floors, empty ceiling. Just a human desert.

AUGUST. There was a coat hook on the back of the door . . .

ERIC. Threw it out.

AUGUST. Good. (*a beat*)

JUNE. I'm going home for the war, what are you going to do?

ERIC. Make money.

JUNE. How? You're going in the Army.

ERIC. I'm going into procurement. Hey, August — you've been a great roomie, pal.

AUGUST. Thanks. (*a beat*)

JUNE. I haven't seen my folks in a long time. It'll be weird being at home again. Still, I saw a movie once about women back in some other war, and they stayed at home and they had fun.

RUSSELL. (*Entering*) How 'bout your clothes?

AUGUST. Burn 'em.

RUSSELL. Ones you got on?

AUGUST. I'll hang on to those.

RUSSELL. (*picking up another box*) Suit yourself. (*RUSSELL Exits.*)

ERIC. "No generation has been as ready for war as this one." That's what my history prof said today. The kids all smiled. They think he's a faggot.

JUNE. Is he?

ERIC. He is if he thinks like that. You know what I did? I stood right up and said, "We are about to fight for the delicate wasp-waist of the Americas. We are going to keep the Caribbean blue and warm, and keep the volcanoes from exploding." Kids cheered. I wouldn't've done it last semester, but now it doesn't matter.

JUNE. What'd he say then?

ERIC. He was floored. There was nothing he could say. He just squeezed out Santayana's old road apple about "Those who forget the past are doomed to repeat it," and I said, "Well, *thank God!* Thank God someone's bright enough to repeat the past." You know why?

JUNE. Why?

ERIC. 'Cause those who don't repeat the past are doomed to forget it.

RUSSELL. (*Entering*) It's all in the car. You want to light it?

AUGUST. In a minute.

RUSSELL. Got a full tank of gas. Think it's far enough away from the house.

JUNE. The Chinese say, "May you live in interesting times." I think these are interesting times.

ERIC. Bet your ass. Do you have any idea how much money we made after our last successful war? Twenty-five years of unprecedented economic growth. And it'll be *best* for our enemies. Look at Germany and Japan.

RUSSELL. I want to go down there and stand a certain way. That's all I want to do. I want to stand a certain way in the jungle.

(*Slowly lights fade back to the original spot on AUGUST.*)

AUGUST. My mistake was exiling the dogs from the classroom. I go back over and over it in my mind. If I had . . . not frozen. If instead I had moved down under the table, *with* the dogs. With the bitch's terrified shrieks, the male's frantic, reflexive movements—all the pitiful, ancient . . . heat of it. If I'd let the students go instead. Stayed alone with the dogs, waiting till they'd finished.

RUSSELL. (*from the darkness*) Hey August—when you light the car, you want to be in or out?

AUGUST. In. (*Spot out suddenly*)

THE END

Cameras

by
Jon Jory

CAMERAS by Jon Jory

CAST

Photographers:*   ACTOR ONE
                    ACTOR TWO
                    ACTOR THREE
                    ACTOR FOUR
                    ACTOR FIVE
                    ACTOR SIX

Person with Roses
Dancers in Evening Dress
Male Stripper
Man with Dropcloth and Gun
Pregnant Woman
Young Woman
Man with a Water Pistol

*The photographers may be played by any combination of men and women that is desired.

240

Cameras

by

Jon Jory

Six actors with cameras sit and stand about the stage. These six may be in any combination of men and women that is desired. They are dressed in a low-key combination of black, brown, blue and gray. Some are cleaning lenses, loading film, and dry focusing. No one, at the beginning, is actually taking photos.

The dialogue of the photographers is purposely not highly defined. They are professionals with ideas about their profession. In a way, they seem very much the same.

ACTOR ONE. There are people who love the technology. I have a friend who has fifty thousand dollars worth of lenses; thirty, forty cameras; a completely outfitted shop for his own repairs. Not me. For me, it's a point of honor, I don't care about the mechanism, the way it works, how you take it apart, put it together. Listen, I don't consider that the point. What I care about is the image, okay? Remember when there used to be F-stops? I lost a hundred pictures I couldn't afford to lose because I was fiddling with those F-stops. Ideally, I'd take the picture with my eyes, and the print would come out of my mouth. The rest of it just doesn't matter to me.

ACTOR TWO. High relief. I can't get enough of it. I'm a junkie for high relief. Black blacks, white whites. Black on white. White on black. The kind of thing you see in the newspapers on a slow news day. Construction workers silhouetted against the sky twenty stories up. You've seen it. With these lacework cranes in the background. Low detail work, because the more detail the less sense you have of the image as a whole. I want to take it in like a breath or a swallow. I don't want you looking at this bit or that bit. I want you looking at the whole thing.

(Someone comes out with three roses, tosses them casually onto the floor and Exits. One photographer bends to rearrange them.)

241

ACTOR THREE. No.

ACTOR FOUR. Why no?

ACTOR THREE. Shoot them like they are.

ACTOR FOUR. (*reaching*) Just this one.

ACTOR THREE. No. Let it be what it is. Leave the image alone. See what you get.

ACTOR FOUR. What I'll get will be no composition.

ACTOR THREE. Bingo. What I want is no composition. What I long for is no composition. It just drives me crazy. Control, control, control, control. I feel like I'll cash it in if I see one more indescribably manipulated, absolutely predictable, unbelievably arrogant, monumentally balanced composition.

ACTOR TWO. What you want is a rush. The composition's hidden inside the rush.

(*A couple in evening dress foxtrot on. Slick ballroom dancing. No music. Actor Five and a couple of others photograph them.*)

ACTOR FIVE. Good. Good. Better. Much better. You can't catch this stuff and think at the same time. You have to get your head out of your way if you want to do this. Great. Good. There is only one thing in this world a camera can do that the eye can't, and that is to stop movement. Bam! Bam! Think about it. If there was no movement you wouldn't need a photographer, you could bring people out on a bus to see it.

ACTOR THREE. Except for the light.

ACTOR SIX. Stopping the movement is commonplace. Stopping the movement is just what the camera does. Breaking down the image, lifting out part of the whole, making the selection. Choosing, as my post-modern friends might say, what isn't there . . . like the feet, love the feet, come here, feet. You may have seen dancing, but you ain't seen my feet.

ACTOR THREE. Freeze.

(*The dancers stop-action by the roses.*)

You want to know how this works? This one right here? If you take an inanimate object . . . the roses . . . and you put a human being in the same frame, what happens? The viewer makes a story. Why did the dancers drop the flowers? Doomed love. They're dancing and one of them asks for a divorce! Really! The fact is, and this is a fact, that the viewer will either make a story out of the frame or they will reject the image. Reject it cold. You cannot, no matter how hard you try, make a meaningless picture. I'm telling you they will invent the meaning. You never have a picture, you have an interpretation of a picture.

(*The dancers dance off with photographers snapping and, at the same time, a young man saunters on. He is stripped to the waist, wearing jeans. In slow motion he takes them off.*)

ACTOR TWO. Patterns. That's all it really it. Music has chords, a photograph has patterns. You know, you get right down to it, it's all just dots.

ACTOR ONE. (*taking pictures of the strip*) Well, it's not technology.

ACTOR FOUR. Engineering maybe.

ACTOR SIX. The hard sell.

ACTOR FOUR. How about two minutes of complete quiet to let me get off on this.

ACTOR FIVE. They don't see what you shoot anyway.

ACTOR TWO. Turn around . . .

ACTOR SIX. Slowwwwwwwwwly.

ACTOR ONE. Over here.

ACTOR FIVE. They see ahead of the picture, or past it. The guy they see has no clothes on. The guy they see is touching them. They don't even see him, they feel him. They walk right through the picture into their own heads.

ACTOR SIX. End of a role.

ACTOR THREE. Got it.

ACTOR TWO. GOT IT.

ACTOR FOUR. Forget it.

(*The model walks off and is passed by a man in a business suit with dark glasses and a briefcase carrying a see-through plastic drop cloth still in its hardware store package.*)

ACTOR FOUR. The only thing left to do is get incredibly small, infinitesimally small.

(*The man opens the drop cloth and carefully spreads it out on the white floor covering.*)

ACTOR ONE. (*looking at the man*) No opportunity.

(*The man opens his briefcase, takes out a sheet and moves* U.S.
  where he hangs it over a wire stretched across the stage.)

ACTOR SIX. Small is right. Smaller than small. Some part of a
part of a part that can't be seen with the naked eye. Micro photography
that's the only frontier. The only thing nobody's seen.
  ACTOR TWO. The only image that isn't used up.
  ACTOR SIX. We're talking hair follicles here, we're talking dust
mote mites living on an elephant hide, blown up so they look like
whatever scared the shit out of you while it ate the world in the
fifties monster movies.

(*The man sits down on the drop cloth and opens the briefcase from
  which he takes a disassembled pistol. He professionally puts
  it together.*)

See, I don't buy that storytelling stuff because there isn't a story
left they haven't heard, not a variation of a story left. People are
bored stiff with their minds, you haven't noticed? Mother, son,
death, war, baby, redemption, love, separation. One giant, congealed,
lump of a story. Rule one: you only want what you
haven't seen before.

(*A pregnant women Enters; she poses smelling a small spring
  bouquet.*)

ACTOR THREE. You have got to be kidding.

(*She Exits. The man takes out a handful of cartridges and loads
  the pistol. Two photographers focus on him.*)

ACTOR FOUR. (*casting a critical eye on him*) I don't know,
maybe.
  ACTOR ONE. Stand over behind the guy.
  ACTOR TWO. Why?
  ACTOR ONE. Because it's a photo opportunity, okay?

(*The man on the drop cloth clicks the gun closed. He sights along
  it. He puts it down. He takes a white apron out of the briefcase,
  stands up, and puts it on.*)

ACTOR TWO. The guy shooting the guy shooting, right?

ACTOR THREE. The guy shooting the guy shooting the guy shooting.

(*The photographers move in shooting each other and the guy. The man sits down again on the drop cloth.*)

ACTOR FIVE. So we've seen all the events but we haven't seen all the people seeing the events?

ACTOR ONE. There is no activity . . . you're in my way . . . no activity you can find or imagine . . . over here, please . . . that has any moral force or essential interest other than the emotion it contains. If it's passionate, you can see it a thousand times.

(*The man on the drop cloth puts the business end of the pistol in his mouth. The photographers shoot.*)

ACTOR THREE. All you've got is the act and the viewer. The act *and* the viewer.

ACTOR FIVE. Otherwise, it's a knife that doesn't cut.

(*A young woman in a simple dress Enters. The others freeze photographing the man on the drop cloth. Another man Enters carrying an elaborate automatic water pistol and stands by the sheet hanging on the wire.*)

YOUNG WOMAN. I was driving through West Virginia and ahead of me I saw where this car had lost control and run through a road crew working on a road divider. The car had hit some kind of road equipment . . . a dredger, a digger, a dozer . . . I don't know what it was. Other cars had stopped, a police car, a couple of others. I thought . . . I didn't know . . . if I could help or . . . so I got out. Over on . . . by the divider there were two men kneeling by a guy . . . I guess from the crew. His leg was out at this angle, and he was rolling back and forth, back and forth, and they were . . . I don't know . . . They were restraining him, trying to, but he wasn't making a sound. And over at this car, the one that hit the equipment, there were these men and a woman in a red coat, contorted, trying with their hands to wrench the car door open and this man behind the wheel screaming, screaming like he never took a breath. I know it's impossible, but the sound was continuous. And I went . . . went over . . . and men motioned me . . . you know, to pull to . . . one was on top of the car, another had this, a coat bundled, wrapped around his hand pounding the window, breaking it in . . . all of us . . . and there was like this roaring of effort, the sound of this incredible physical effort, and the screaming. And I could . . . while we . . . I could see away from the car this guy, through the screaming, taking pictures. Pictures of the guy on the ground, pictures of us. Thirty feet away. And every time I think of this, every time I wonder, wonder if one more pair of hands . . . after awhile he stopped screaming.

(*There is the sound of a gunshot. The man by the white sheet shoots red liquid from the water pistol onto its surface. The man on the dropcloth tumbles clumsily over. The photographers take pictures of him. The lights dim. They are shooting with flash now.*)

YOUNG WOMAN. Wouldn't it be better to throw the fucking camera . . . get it out of the way. Yell a warning, rip things open, smother the flames, catch the child, try whatever. Wouldn't it be better.

(*The flashes stop.*)

I have this theory about the indecency of art. Being out of life. Making money from it, getting off on it. Taking pictures of it so we can all be properly horrified . . . and safe. I'd like to be wrong, but I don't think I am.

(*There is one camera flash in the dark. Then it's over.*)

The End